PrincetonReview.com

GRAMMAR SMART JUNIOR

Good Grammar Made Easy

by Liz Buffa, Jane Mallison,
and The Staff of The Princeton Review

3rd Edition

Random House, Inc.,
New York

The Princeton Review, Inc.
2315 Broadway
New York, NY 10024
Email: bookeditor@review.com

ISBN 978-0-375-42870-8

Publisher: Robert Franek
Editor: Adrinda Kelly
Director of Production: Scott Harris
Senior Production Editor: M. Tighe Wall

Printed in the United States of America.

10 9 8 7 6 5 4 3 2 1

ACKNOWLEDGMENTS

Liz Buffa would like to thank the following for their invaluable contributions: Michael Freedman, Marcia Lerner, Diane Fagiola, and Marissa La Magna for their emotional support. And thanks of course to Dominick, David, and Paul, for their patience and proofreading.

Jane Mallison gratefully acknowledges the memory of Miss Grace Elmore, the most influential of early teachers. Thanks to Karl Beason for his support of projects like this one. And continuing thanks to that wizard of words and sentences (and daily life), Kenneth Silverman.

CONTENTS

INTRODUCTION

WHY SHOULD I LEARN ABOUT GRAMMAR?

Some of you are great with fashion, some of you are great at reading, and some of you are great at making lay-ups on the basketball court. But no matter what your skills are and what you like the most, you—like everybody else—have to talk to people and write from time to time. (That's a no-brainer, right?) Communication is important, and using proper grammar is also important, for two reasons: to be clear and to sound educated. Huh?

Let us explain. Many of the grammar rules you will encounter can make your life easier. You need to communicate with people, right? Well, let's say you write this in a paper:

> **"I told Maria that I like Nickelback's new CD more than her."**

Now, did you just insult your friend by saying that you like a CD more than you like her? Or did you just say that you like this particular CD more than she likes it? Well, according to the rules of formal grammar, you told her that you like this CD more than you like her, and that's probably not what you meant.

That's the first way that grammar helps you—if you use your words carefully and correctly, you can avoid misunderstandings.

NOW, ABOUT THE SOUNDING EDUCATED PART . . .

Sure, we want you to speak and write perfectly all the time because there is beauty in doing so. Would you be amazed to know that the word *glamour* comes directly from the word *grammar*? (It's true! Check it out in the dictionary.) In medieval times, a spellbinding wizard seemed to possess the knowledge to perform magic with words. Even today, those who have power over words possess an attractive strength, whether they're writing a report for history class, a legal brief, a movie script, or a love letter.

No matter how insightful your thoughts are, if they're presented with lots of grammatical errors, your paper won't be effective—and you won't get a good grade. And no matter how qualified an applicant you are, if you go into a job interview years from now and say,

> **"I just know I done good on that test you gave me, sir!"**

Well, you won't be getting that job. Knowing proper grammar is important for many reasons.

WELL, WHAT'S THIS BOOK ABOUT?

We want to teach you good grammar and make it clear, easy, and, most of all, interesting. We don't necessarily expect you to read this book from cover to cover; some of you will just use it for reference when you have a specific question. That's fine. We'll remind you from time to time which really important rules you should always follow no matter what, and which rules are the ones that only English teachers will give you a hard time about. (Like that last sentence. It ends in a preposition and nobody cares.)

BUT I'VE NEVER LIKED GRAMMAR . . .

That's okay. Just give it another chance. Studying grammar can be boring, and it doesn't help when you are asked to speak one way, but often hear English spoken in a completely different way. That's confusing. When you watch TV, read magazines, surf the Internet, and listen to music, you are constantly exposed to grammar that's considered "nonstandard," or just downright "bad."

Now don't get us wrong. We have nothing against "bad grammar" in things like music or advertising. Sometimes using the wrong word sounds better when you're writing lyrics to a song or jingle. (Sometimes the idea is to "sound wrong"—and if there's no "right," you can't get the desired effect of sounding "wrong!" The Rolling Stones probably wouldn't have had their incredible success if Mick Jagger had sung "I Can't Get Any Satisfaction.") But since you aren't a famous rock star (yet), we're going to help you learn the basics about grammar and usage that you need for school and for the more formal situations in life. This kind of knowledge can help you write better school reports and get higher scores on tests, because nonstandard or "bad" grammar is not valued in those situations.

TESTS?

Sure, tests. Even if you haven't had them yet, pretty soon you'll be called upon to answer questions about grammar. Your teacher may ask you to identify a dependent clause or to find the errors in a poorly written sentence. Both of these tasks will be simple if you start now by developing an ear for good grammar. What does that mean? If you have an ear for music, you may recognize immediately if a song is by Gwen Stefani or Nelly Furtado. If you have an ear for good grammar, your "inner ear" will detect when something just doesn't sound right.

BUT WAIT A MINUTE... MY COMPUTER HAS A GRAMMAR CHECKER AND A SPELL-CHECKER!

Grammar checkers and spell-checkers exist on most word processing programs. Some silly people now believe that there will be no reason for kids to learn grammar and spelling in the future, because it will simply be a matter of hitting a key and letting the computer change your wonderful—yet grammatically incorrect—thoughts into perfect, sparkling English. Well, we hate to break it to you, but it's not that simple.

Really. Would we lie to you? Spell-checkers will pick up many misspellings, but first you have to spell a word sort of right for a spell-checker to correct it. If you're way off, it won't know which word you're aiming for. (It is only a machine, after all.) And it won't pick up misspellings in which you turn one word into another (for example, if you spell *you're* as *your*). Both are correctly spelled words, and the spell-checker picks out only those words that don't appear in its dictionary. And those grammar checkers? Forget them. As of now, they are pretty much useless.

If you tried to use a grammar checker on a report or essay, chances are you'd be more lost after you were done than before you started.

HOW TO USE THIS BOOK:
THREE MAJOR SECTIONS

This book is arranged so that it will be easy to follow and fun to read. The first section of the book is designed to cover the basic collection of words and terms that you need in your brain in order to talk easily about words and sentences. The second section begins to move from the "in-your-head" kind of learning to the concrete, "hands-on" type of knowledge you can apply immediately. The third section is even more "hands-on," as it covers common errors, sentence diagramming, spelling, and punctuation. It also offers good suggestions for further reading that will reinforce your grammar knowledge.

In all three sections, you can read a little bit at a time and test yourself with the quizzes that follow each topic. They are there for you to figure out if you have truly mastered the concept being presented. You don't have to get every question right to feel good about yourself. If you get most of the questions right on the quizzes, you're doing well. To help you practice your new knowledge of grammar and usage, you'll find a series of short passages featuring characters from Greek mythology. (If you've already studied a little mythology in school, you'll meet some old friends. If you haven't yet encountered any of these myths in school, you'll get an introduction here that will put you ahead of the game later on.)

Those of you who open the book only to find an answer to a specific question will appreciate that we go in order, from basic definitions to more detailed points of grammar to common errors and tips. You may find yourself reading a little bit ahead just to see how things really work in this complicated machine we call grammar. It's not so bad after all—and when you're done, you'll be rewarded with the ability to speak and write well. After all, a side effect of being educated is that you sound educated!

PART 1

Basic Knowledge:
The Names of Things

CHAPTER 1
The Parts of Speech

To learn about grammar you have to learn the names of things. The parts of speech are the words you use to put sentences and paragraphs together. To put them together properly, you need to know what each word is called and what role it plays.

So what's the point? Well, we won't fool you. Chances are good that, unless you become a contestant on *Are You Smarter Than a 5th Grader?* in your adult life, you won't be called upon regularly to name the parts of speech. So do we really care if you can name the parts of speech with your eyes closed? No, not really. We are defining these terms so that you will understand what we are talking about throughout the book. And chances are that, as a student, you will need to know these terms when your teacher gives you one of those pesky pop quizzes.

If you play baseball, you don't really need to know the name of a squeeze play to be able to make one, right? And you don't need to know the name of a reflexive pronoun to use one properly. But if you look up at your coach blankly when he asks you to make a squeeze play, he may think, "Hey, I'm not sure if this kid really knows how to play baseball." So, this section is the beginning of the "in-your-head" grammar knowledge that you hardly thought you knew.

Let's get started. Words are put into eight different categories, depending upon the roles they play in sentences. Here are the names of the eight parts of speech:

nouns
pronouns
verbs
adjectives
adverbs
prepositions
conjunctions
interjections

If you are confused, the easiest way to find out the part of speech of a word is to look up the word in a dictionary. A dictionary definition will include information about the word's what part of speech. For example:

fly, n.; pl. **flies**. 1. a housefly; any of a group of insects with two transparent wings, including the housefly and the Mayfly. 2. a device made of feathers, silk, etc., to resemble an insect, used in fishing as a bait.

Now, as you can see, this is the definition of *fly* that means an insect or fishing lure. That little "n." after the word tells you that *fly* is a noun, and the "pl." tells you that the plural of *fly* is *flies*. It gives you two definitions. (In many dictionaries the first definition is the most common use of the word.) But there's another definition of *fly* that means something completely different.

fly, v.; **flew**, pt.; **flown**, pp. 1. to move through the air, with wings, as a bird flies, or by airplane. 2. to operate an airplane. 3. to float in the air, as a kite or flag does.

TIP
The same word may have many different parts of speech.

This definition of *fly* indicates that *fly* can also be a verb. It also gives you some of the different tenses of the verb. (We'll get to those later in Chapter 4.)

If we asked you to tell us the part of speech of, say, the word *well*, the correct answer would be "I can't tell." Let's look at some sentences.

> The peasant carried the water from the **well**. (noun)
> Tears began to **well** up in the official's eyes. (verb)
> You should read this chapter in the science book really **well**. (adverb)
> It's more fun to be a **well** person than to be a sick person. (adjective)
> **Well**, I'm glad to see you here today! (interjection)

But we're getting ahead of the game. For now, you should know that some words may only, and always, be one part of speech; others, though, may be used as more than one part of speech depending on the way they are used in a sentence—what we call the context.

NOUNS

A **noun** is a person, place, thing, or idea.

Person: Pierre, Juanita, firefighter, friend, Mom
Place: school, home, Blue Horizon Diner
Thing: cat, calendar, MP3, DVD
Idea: truth, justice, liberty

There are two general categories of nouns: common nouns and proper nouns.

A common noun is a word that names a type of person, place, or thing. A proper noun names a specific person, place, or thing. Compare the two:

Common noun	Proper noun
girl	Maria
teacher	Mr. Escobar
city	Chicago
state	Alaska
college	Michigan State

What do you notice about common nouns and proper nouns? Proper nouns are always capitalized and common nouns are not (unless, of course, they begin a sentence).

In the following paragraph, the nouns are in italics.

> *Jem* stayed moody and silent for a *week*. As *Atticus* had once advised me to do, I tried to climb into *Jem's skin* and walk around in it: if I had not gone to the *Radley Place* at two in the *morning*, my *funeral* would have been held the next *afternoon*. So I left Jem alone and tried not to bother him.
>
> from *To Kill a Mockingbird*, by Harper Lee

QUIZ #1: NOUNS

Underline all the common nouns in the following passage and circle all the proper nouns. Check your answers at the back of the book.

Zeus, the leader of the Greek gods, was sitting on his ebony throne at the top of Mt. Olympus. In his hand he was holding a jagged thunderbolt, which made him look powerful. But the truth is that he was feeling a little lonely and wanted some companionship, so he called for his brother.

"Yo, Poseidon!" he called in an ungodlike way. "Are you still the king of the sea?"

"Oh, brother," said Poseidon. "You know it's a lifetime position. I wear seaweed in my hair. The mermaids are my royal subjects. I sleep with the fishes."

"Just checking," said the king of the gods, adjusting the angle of his thunderbolt toward southern Greece. "Where's the goddess of love?"

Aphrodite glided forward in a chariot pulled by pea-cocks. "The world of romance is getting ready for Valentine's Day. I'm teaching Cupid to cut hearts out of red paper, but he keeps trying to do it with his blind-fold on. That boy!"

"Hmm, Valentine's Day," mused Zeus quietly. "That makes me think of birthdays. I'd better start thinking of a gift for Hera's birthday. Last year I forgot, and she threw a Grecian urn at me."

PRONOUNS

Okay, now that you know what a noun is, you'll be able to recognize pronouns. **Pronouns** are used as stand-ins for nouns—sort of like stunt people for actors in a movie. Think of how horrible and awkward your sentences would sound without pronouns to stand in for nouns every now and then. For example, instead of saying,

> Marcia told John that Marcia liked John's story better than Marcia liked Marcia's story.

you get to say,

> Marcia told John that she liked his story better than she liked hers.

Obviously, pronouns make your sentences a little smoother. Using them means you don't have to repeat the nouns over and over again, when we all know what noun you're referring to. The italicized words in the following paragraph are pronouns.

> *We* lived on the main residential street in town—Atticus, Jem and *I*, plus Calpurnia, our cook. Jem and *I* found our father satisfactory: *he* played with *us*, read to *us*, and treated *us* with courteous detachment.
>
> from *To Kill a Mockingbird*, by Harper Lee

Note
All the pronouns that we've looked at so far are personal pronouns. Most of them replace the nouns used for people, but the pronouns it and they and them can replace nouns used for places or things. As you go further in this book, you'll learn about other types of pronouns, but you're off to a good start with your knowledge of personal pronouns, because they are by far the most common.

Underline the pronouns in the following passage. Check your answers at the back of the book.

Zeus came out of his trance of thinking about Hera's birthday. He saw Poseidon looking at his wristwatch. Aphrodite looked as if she were impatient. "They are all waiting for me to speak," he realized.

"Okay," Zeus said briskly. "We all need to think hard. Does Hera need an iPod? Would she prefer more perfume? I know she likes frangipani. This gift for her—where can I buy it?"

Aphrodite smiled sweetly at him. "Why don't I have my husband Hephaestus make her a sculpture of some kind? He is a divine blacksmith, you know, and he has made some nifty things. She'll be grateful to me...I mean to us...for this idea."

Poseidon looked at them. "No, too artsy. I think good old-fashioned roses would be better for her. Let's get Hermes to deliver them. After all, he has wings on his hat and on his shoes!"

VERBS

A **verb** is a word that expresses an action or a state of being. A verb is one of the most important words in a sentence—you cannot express a complete thought without one.

The action may be:

Physical: I *ran* through the field.
AJ *played* football on Saturday morning.

Mental: I *thought* you'd be here.
Karl *hoped* for a sunny day.

As a "state of being," a verb expresses what something is, or what its condition is, rather than a mental action.

State of being: Anna *is* happy.
Paul *felt* sick.
The music *sounded* loud.
Valerie *was* successful.
The pizza *tasted* good.

In the following paragraph, all the verbs are in italics.

Lennie *went* behind the tree and *brought* out a litter of dried leaves and twigs. He *threw* them in a heap on the old ash pile and *went* back for more and more. It *was* almost night now. A dove's wings *whistled* over the water. George *walked* to the fire pile and *lighted* the dry leaves. The flame *crackled* up among the twigs and *fell* to work. George *undid* his bundle and *brought* out three cans of beans.

from *Of Mice and Men*, by John Steinbeck

QUIZ #3: VERBS

Underline the verbs in the following passage. Check your answers at the back of the book.

Hermes flew toward the throne of Zeus and landed with an abrupt jolt. He removed his hat with the wings and tucked it under his arm.

"I am at your service, Zeus. I will do your bidding," he said with a polite semi-bow.

"Greetings, Hermes. You will deliver my birthday gift to my wife, Hera. I expect your full cooperation. You should fly with the speed of lightning," he said, as he crinkled his eyebrows in a way that gave him a look of even greater importance.

Hermes wondered why Zeus questioned his speed. After all, he too was a god, not just a flunky who delivered packages. But still it was true that Zeus was more powerful, so he muttered only, "But of course."

"Please see to it that the gift is wrapped in the highest-quality papyrus from the banks of the Nile," said Zeus. "And do not rattle, shake, or drop the box as you are carrying it. Is this clear?"

"Of course. Give me the gift and I will fulfill your commands."

"The gift? Oh, yes. I have decided that flowers are too ordinary, but I have confidence you will think of something."

ADJECTIVES

It would be a dreary world indeed without adjectives. As a matter of fact, it would just be a world, because there'd be no words like *dreary*. Now, you may have thought that nouns, pronouns, and verbs were just okay, but adjectives, well, that's another story. In grammar and writing, the fun really starts when you get to describe things, and that's where adjectives come in. An **adjective** is a word that describes or modifies a noun. In other words, an adjective answers questions about a noun. For example:

> **Noun:** Book—what kind of book is it?
> It is a red book.
> It is a large book.

Noun: House—whose house is it?
It is my house.
[Here, a possessive pronoun acts as an adjective.]
Daisy's house is down the street.

Noun: Computer—which computer is it?
Which computer are you working on?
What computer did you sit at?
This computer is my favorite.
That computer is broken.

(Adjectives can also describe pronouns, but the rules are the same as for nouns.)

Sometimes an adjective that describes the subject can come *after* the verb.

The evening was *cool*.
The book is *red*.
Erick was *creative*.
We were *angry*.

In the following paragraph, all the adjectives are in italics.

He stood frowning as the ring of *blue-white* fire flickered and danced; he even looked *cold*, with a *dark*, *pinched* look round the bones of his face. "They bring in the *deep* cold," he said, half to himself. "The cold of the void, of *black* space. . ."

from *The Dark Is Rising*, by Susan Cooper

Underline all the adjectives you find in this passage. (Treat possessive pronouns such as *my* as adjectives.) Check your answers at the back of the book.

Hermes marveled at Zeus's cocky manner. Why should the delivery god have to decide on the perfect gift? He knew he needed wise advice, so why not go to Athena, the supremely wise goddess of wisdom?

He found her in her cavernous chamber, sitting in front of a large loom. In addition to her great wisdom, Athena was a super-duper weaver, and had once won an important weaving competition with Arachne. Hermes chuckled as he recalled how Athena had transformed Arachne into a big, hairy spider after the contest. He would be very polite to Athena.

"Oh, divine Athena," he began, as he entered the huge room. "Your superior wisdom is needed. What should Zeus give the picky Hera for her birthday?"

ADVERBS

Adverbs are the workhorses of descriptive words. While an adjective describes a noun (or sometimes a pronoun), an **adverb** is a word that describes or modifies a verb, an adjective, or even another adverb. Adverbs answer questions about those verbs, adjectives, or other adverbs. What does that mean? Here are some examples.

> David *always* eats a lot.
> Diane did well *enough* on her exam.

The adverbs above answer the question *how*. The first adverb describes the verb *eats* and tells you *how often* David eats. The second adverb describes the adverb *well* and tells you *how well* Diane did.

> He will be here *later*.
> Mr. Hatcher will arrive *soon*.

The adverbs above answer the question *when*. The first adverb describes the verb *be* and tells you *when* he will be here. The second adverb describes the verb *arrive* and tells you *when* Mr. Hatcher will arrive.

> Evan ran *behind*.
> Mary Beth looked *there*.

These adverbs answer the question *where*. The first one describes the verb *ran* and tells you *where* Evan ran. The

Fun Fact
Greek mythology tells us that Athens was named after the great goddess of wisdom and war, Athena. Athena and Poseidon (god of the ocean) both wanted claim to the city. It was decided that the two gods would present the city with a gift, and the citizens and the other gods would give the island to the better gifter. Poseidon struck the ground with his trident and opened a spring. Athena gave the city an olive tree. The tree offered the people food, shelter, and shade, while the spring offered only saltwater. The city was given to Athena and has been called Athens ever since.

second one describes the verb *looked* and tells you *where* Mary Beth looked.

> I *really, really* want to go to the movies.
> Peter *actually* will go along with me.

These adverbs are used for emphasis. In the first sentence the adverbs emphasize the verb *want*. The adverb in the second sentence emphasizes the verb *go*.

> Dominick runs *swiftly*.
> Deidre sings *happily*.

Adverbs like the ones above are the most common. They end in -*ly* and answer the question *how*. How does Dominick run? *Swiftly*. How does Deidre sing? *Happily*.

Many adverbs end in -*ly*, but, as you can see, many others do not.

QUIZ #5: ADVERBS

Underline all the adverbs you find in the passage below. Check your answers at the back of the book.

"Zeus always gets other gods to do his work!" said Athena crossly. "Can he ever think of anything but himself? Although I am very wise, this is a waste of my wisdom."

Hermes paused and then spoke flatteringly. "I could never be as wise as you. I tried once, but it was impossible."

Athena smiled sweetly, for compliments always pleased her. "Let's see. Maybe I can think of something. Hera is quite vain, I believe. Vain women like her never tire of looking at themselves. Get Hephaestus to cut a round piece of bronze and polish it vigorously. Hera will then be able to see her reflection without having to trek to the royal reflecting pool. Carefully place a gold ornament of an eagle at the top and the bottom. Hera will then be immensely pleased. Now, what shall we call my brilliant new invention?"

Hermes modestly bowed his head in tribute to her genius. "Looking glass," he said quietly.

"Looking glass. That's it!"

PREPOSITIONS

Prepositions are difficult to define, but we're going to try. They show how a noun or pronoun is related to another word in a sentence. They give the relationship of the noun or pronoun in place, direction, or time. A preposition will always appear with a noun or pronoun that acts as its object. (You'll learn more later about prepositional phrases, but it's useful right now to know that a preposition must have a "mate.") For example:

> **Place:** Alice was *at* her desk.
> She was *behind* her friend.

At and *behind* place Alice in relation to her desk and her friend.

> **Direction:** Martha came *from* the pizza parlor.
> I was going *to* the movies.

From and *to* give you the directions that *Martha* and *I* are going in relation to something else (here, the pizza parlor and the movies).

> **Time:** I'd rather go skiing *in* February.
> Melanie will be home *at* 3:00 P.M.

In and *at* both connect the nouns to time—February and 3:00 P.M.

Here are some examples of prepositions.

Place: around, through, over, above, in, after, at, behind, under, on, by
Direction: from, to, away, after, into
Time: before, by, at, after, on, in

Some prepositions—such as about and of—show relationships that may not have anything to do with place, direction, or time.

Preposition or adverb? Some words that are often prepositions can be used as adverbs. It's easy to tell the difference. A preposition will always have an object (the noun or pronoun that answers the question *whom* or *what*); an adverb cannot have an object.

Take a look at these four sentences.

I threw the book *down*. (*Down* is an adverb here.)
The wolf came *down* the chimney. (*Down* is a preposition here.)
I hoped to see him, but he was *out*. (*Out* is an adverb here.)
The bat flew *out* the door of the cabin. (*Out* is a preposition here.)

Underline all the prepositions you find in the passage below. Check your answers at the back of the book.

Hephaestus limped slowly toward his furnace. Where was it? He reached around his workbench and patted the stone floor under it. There was his anvil, and beside it was his burlap sack of metals. He put his left hand in the bag and felt for a round object. He produced a perfect circle of bronze. During the next half hour he polished and polished with his godly rag. Then he looked into it and saw his own fire-reddened face. "Amazing!" he thought. "I'm not crazy about Hera, but this is a wonderful gift for her."

Among his other scraps of metal were fragments of silver and gold. From these he fashioned four small eagles and soldered them onto the edges of the bronze. This was indeed a gift worthy of a goddess. "I'm still glad I'm married to Aphrodite," he thought, "but Athena and I make a great professional team!"

CONJUNCTIONS

A **conjunction** is a joining word. (Think of how a junction is where roads join together.) You might say

> Juanita went to school. She took a test.

You could make those two sentences into one with a conjunction.

> Juanita went to school *and* she took a test.

or even

> Juanita went to school *and* took a test.

Conjunctions are pretty easy to spot. They join two or more things together in a sentence. Some conjunctions work alone.

> Take the dog *and* the cat to the store with you.
> I wanted to bring our goldfish, *but* my mother said no.
> I'll be happy with goldfish *or* snails.
> *Although* I like snails, I prefer goldfish.

(Notice with that last example that conjunctions don't always come between the things they join. *Although* joins a dependent clause *I like snails* to the main clause *I prefer goldfish*. You'll learn more about this later.)

Some conjunctions work in pairs.

> *Neither* Ollie *nor* Stan would have eaten that goldfish!
> *Either* goldfish *or* snails are delicious when cooked with garlic.

Not only garlic, *but also* onions, are necessary when you are preparing such delicacies!

Underline all the conjunctions. (Hint: Two are hard to find—they are like the conjunctions in the sentences above about goldfish.) Check your answers at the back of the book.

The lame but skilled blacksmith took his beautiful and useful creation and wrapped it in a cloth of purple velvet so it wouldn't get broken or cracked. He wanted to show it off, but he knew Zeus was taking a nap. For that matter, neither Aphrodite nor Hermes was around, for they both had made quick trips to earth. (Aphrodite was having her picture painted while she stood—nude!—on a large half-shell, and Hermes was giving endorsements to a scarf company in western Gaul and to his favorite sports team, the Trojan Horses.)

Was what happened next chance or fate? Hephaestus spotted not only Artemis, the goddess of hunting, with her bow and arrow, but also her twin, Apollo, that versatile chap who was god of both music and healing.

Hephaestus shouted, "Look at my new invention!" for he was very proud of it.

Artemis set down her weapons and shushed the hound that accompanied her. "I love it!" she cried. "Can I have it? I can use it to look behind me when I hunt. Then no crafty boar or sly bear will be able to sneak up on me."

"Actually, Sister," said Apollo, "Hephaestus should give it—or even sell it—to me. My chariot could use a rear-view looking glass."

"No way," said Hephaestus with certainty. "This is headed for Hera, the goddess-who-must-be-obeyed, and for no one else!"

INTERJECTIONS

Hey! Yo! Cool! It's interjection time. Interjections are easy and fun and have no real rules, which makes them especially great. An **interjection** is a word that often stands alone. You add it for emphasis.

> *Wow!* What a great new haircut.
> *Yecch!* You look stupid.
> *Ha!* What do you know about it?

Not all interjections are followed by exclamation points. Sometimes, words that act like introductions are considered interjections. For example:

Really, you should cut your hair.

Yes, you are right.

Underline all the interjections you find in the passage below. Check your answers at the back of the book.

The Great Day Arrives

Wow! What a sight the Great Hall of Olympus was! Streamers of gold and silver (that's real gold and silver) festooned the room. All of the gods of Mt. Olympus had gathered for Hera's birthday party, and, man, were they having a good time! When they had finished playing Pin the Tail on the Centaur (alas, the blindfolded Cupid had almost pinned the tail on Hera herself) and had eaten their nectar-and-ambrosia birthday cake, Zeus was ready to hand over his birthday surprise—the first looking glass ever known to men (or gods).

Hermes, who was responsible for getting the present to the party, was panicking. "Yikes! Where did I put that package? Oh no! Did Apollo forget to return it after he examined it? Eek!" He glanced frantically around the Great Hall, furrowing his brow. Aha! There it was on the mantel, over the great fireplace. "Yes!" he cried, pumping his fist in the air and handing the velvet-covered box to Zeus.

"By Hercules," muttered Zeus. "I was afraid you'd forgotten it." Then he kissed Hera on the cheek and said, "Well, well, I guess it's time for a little gift."

Hera pulled back the soft wrapping and saw the shining brass circle with its eagle ornamentation. "Oh my," she said, "this is beautiful!" And when she held it up to her face and realized it held her reflection, she shouted, "Yippee! Now I can admire my beauty whenever I like. You've made me very happy, Zeus."

Her husband thought, "Zounds! I've managed to please her. Hip, hip, hooray for the creative team of Athena and Hephaestus!"

Party On with Parts of Speech

Okay, you've finished learning about the parts of speech. Now you can play the parts-of-speech games. You'll need a friend or two. Ask each person to call out a word that is the part of speech required in each blank. Don't tell your friends the title or the subject of the story. The more creative the words are, the funnier the final story will be. Read the story aloud once all the blanks are filled in.

PARTS-OF-SPEECH GAME #1: CANDY WARNING

Warning: Candy Can Be Hazardous to Your Health

Washington, D.C.—The National Health Department released a (noun) _____ warning young (plural noun) _____ about the dangers of (verb ending in –ing) _____ candy. "Many people don't realize that candy contains (noun) _____ ," warned a senior official at the department.

"If you eat (adjective) _____ candy three or more times a (noun) _____, you will jeopardize your chances of growing up (adjective) _____." "(interjection) _____!" proclaimed a group of (nouns) _____. "We love to (verb) _____ candy. We (verb) _____ it almost once a day!"

To minimize the danger, officials advise that you (verb) _____ your candy (adverb) _____ and (verb) _____ immediately (preposition) _____ your house.

PARTS-OF-SPEECH GAME #2:
SCHOOL SURVIVAL GUIDE

If you want to make it through a (noun) _____ at school, you should always remember to (verb) _____ your teachers. If you (verb) _____ your (adjective) _____ teachers, you can expect to (verb) _____ every single time.

How do you (verb) _____ time and time again? (interjection) _____! Call your teacher a (noun) _____ and (singular pronoun) _____ will really (verb) _____ your effort. Another surefire way to (verb) _____ your (adjective) teacher is to (adverb) _____ (verb) _____ that teacher in front of the whole (group noun) _____.

PARTS-OF-SPEECH GAME #3:
A Trip to the Moon

Are you interested in (verb ending in -*ing*) _____ to the moon? Well, you will need a/an (adjective) _____ (noun) _____ and your favorite (noun) _____. Take these things and (verb) them together in your best (noun). "(interjection) _____!" you may say, "Is that all I need to (verb) _____ to the moon?"

"(interjection) _____" is what I say to you. All it takes is a couple of (nouns) _____ and a few very (adjective) _____ (nouns) _____ and soon you'll be (adverb) _____ on your way! Bon voyage!

Review

There are eight parts of speech. Give a quick definition and an example of each one. The answers are on pages 268–269.

1. _____

2. _____

3. _____

4. _____

5. _____

6. _____

7. _____

8. _____

END-OF-CHAPTER REVIEW

Now that you've named the parts of speech, can you identify them in a sentence? In each of the following sentences, identify the part of speech above each word. Use *N* for noun, *P* for pronoun, *V* for verb, *ADJ* for adjective, *ADV* for adverb, *PR* for preposition, *C* for conjunction, and *I* for interjection. A few are tricky, but don't get discouraged.

1. Demeter, goddess of agriculture, spent six months of the year with her daughter.

2. Persephone spent the other six months with her husband, Hades.

3. He lived beneath the earth; his two brothers proudly ruled the earth and the sea.

4. He was very sad when Persephone left in the spring and always cried, "Alas!"

5. The Greeks believed spring and summer came with Persephone's return.

CHAPTER 2
The Sentence and Its Parts

Now that you know the parts of speech, let's talk about how sentences are put together. The parts of speech play different roles in different sentences. There are two main parts of a sentence. They are the **subject** and the **predicate**.

Why should you care about this? That's simple: because there must be a subject and a predicate in a complete sentence. Look at the following examples.

> **Not a sentence:** John and Mary.
> **Not a sentence:** Went to the store.
> **A sentence:** John and Mary went to the store.

But do you always speak in complete sentences? No way! There are plenty of times when, for creative purposes, you may use only a fragment, or a piece of a sentence, to make your point. But if you are using fragments when you should be using full, complete sentences (in formal writing, for example), you may want to learn how to be more effective.

THE SUBJECT

If your friend asked you what the subject of the book you were reading was, you'd tell her what the book was about, right? Well, the subject of a sentence is simply what the sentence is about. The easiest way to find the subject of a sentence is to find the verb (action word), and then ask yourself who or what is doing that action. For example, look at this sentence.

Bob ran in the race.

What is the verb? *Ran.* Who ran? *Bob. Bob* is the subject of the sentence.

Not all subjects come first in a sentence.

After running in the race, Brenda was exhausted.

What is the verb? *Was exhausted.* Who was exhausted? *Brenda. Brenda* is the subject of the sentence.

Some sentences have more than one set of subjects and verbs. Check out this one.

While Mike was painting, Grace was writing her paper.

There are two actions in this sentence—painting and writing. Who was painting? *Mike. Mike* is the subject of the first half of the sentence. Who was writing? *Grace. Grace* is the subject of the second half.

There is *always* a subject in a sentence. Sometimes, however, you don't hear or see the subject. These subjects are implied. What does it mean to imply something? It means that you don't say it straight out, but it's what you mean. Saying "I guess you didn't study for this exam" is a teacher's way of implying that you didn't do that well, right?

So what is an implied subject? Look at this example.

Get out of here!

This sentence is a complete thought. And how do you figure out the subject? Well, just as before, ask yourself these questions. What is the verb? *Get out.* Who is supposed to get out? Well, sorry, but you are. The subject here is *you.* In other words, the speaker is implying this.

You **get out of here!**

Sometimes, then, when a speaker is directing a comment right at someone, he won't say *you,* but *you* is implied. It's understood. Here are more examples of an implied subject. You'll notice all these understood subjects come in imperative sentences, sentences that make a command or a request.

> **Please turn off the television.**
> **Don't eat that ice cream.**
> **Wait until 4:30.**

Sometimes, there are words between the subject and the verb; don't let these throw you off. For example:

> Mary, the best student in class, was awarded the blue ribbon.

Who was awarded? *Mary*—so *Mary* is the subject. The phrase *the best student in class* describes Mary. Now look at the following sentence.

> One of the boys was going to give the speech.

This is a little trickier. Who is giving the speech? Not boys, but *one of the boys*. *One*—a pronoun—is the subject. When you are looking for the subject, try to ignore the words that are describing it. It's also good to remember that the subject is never part of a prepositional phrase, and you probably recognized *of the boys* as a prepositional phrase. Look for the verb and ask yourself who or what is performing the action.

QUIZ #9: SUBJECTS

Underline the subject in each of the following sentences. Check your answers at the back of the book.

1. The Romans gave the name "Jupiter" to Zeus.

2. Hera was called "Juno" by them.

3. You can probably guess the Roman name of Aphrodite, goddess of love.

4. Her Roman name was Venus. Were you right?

5. Most speakers of English think of her of Venus.

SIMPLE SUBJECTS AND COMPLETE SUBJECTS

Just for Kicks
What is a seven letter word that let's you spell out seven complete words in the same order their letters appear in the original word? The answer is "therein," which can be broken down into there, the, he, her, here, rein, and in.

Sometimes subjects consist of more than one word. Not all of the words are equally important. Here's where we make a distinction between the simple subject and the complete subject. The **simple subject** is the most important word in a subject. It will be a noun or a pronoun. The **complete subject** includes the simple subject and all of that words and phrases that modify it.

Sometimes the subject is modified by adjectives. Look at the sentence below.

The hyper young cat ran around the house.

Who ran around the house? The *cat*. The words *hyper* and *young* are modifying the word *cat*. The simple subject is *cat*. The complete subject is *The hyper young cat*.

Underline each verb and circle the complete subject that goes with it. Check your answers at the back of the book.

Ares, the god of war, needed some soldiers. He wanted more than a few good men—this powerful god wanted several good men. This god with the bronze helmet knew about the future. There would be a talented mortal with the name of Homer. Someday, this Homer would write a great poem about Greek soldiers. This poet with the sublime style would tell of the Greeks' defeat of the Trojans in the Trojan War. The Greek god of war wanted the Greeks to look very brave and very clever in Homer's poem. The current Greek army and its descendents in future years must be very unusual fighters.

What will this long poem of the future say about the Greeks? This poem of 24 books will show their bravery and will also show their cleverness. The Trojans and their ruler, King Priam, are also very brave. But these Trojans with their long spears lack the outrageous cleverness of the Greeks. This poem, *The Iliad*, must depict the Greeks at their best. And so a crafty man named Odysseus is very interesting to the god of war on his quest.

THE PREDICATE

What is the predicate? Sometimes the verb (whether one word or a verb phrase such as *was running*) is called a **simple predicate**. The **complete predicate** includes the verb as well as the words related to it that complete the thought in the sentence. It's the part of the sentence that tells more about the subject. It describes what the subject does or has. It can also tell what the subject is like. And it includes any adverbs or prepositional phrases that describe the verb.

Let's summarize. The complete predicate includes all the words in the predicate of a sentence. The simple predicate is the main word in the predicate. It is always a verb or verb phrase.

The easiest way to find the predicate is to do your subject search. (Where's the verb? Who or what is the verb talking about?) The verb and (usually) the rest of the sentence is the predicate. Take a look at some simple examples.

Subject	Predicate
Jake	was a man.
He	was nice to everybody.

Don't think, because of these simple examples, that the subject always comes first and that the predicate always comes second. That's probably the easiest way to write sentences, but it would be boring if all sentences were constructed that way.

Sentences should be varied in good writing. That means that some sentences will be long and intricate, while others will be short and simple. Varying sentences in this way makes a piece of writing far more interesting to read. Let's look at a more complicated sentence and find the subject and the predicate.

> **Throughout the history of the school, thousands of kids have walked these halls.**

The verb of this sentence is *have walked*. Who or what have walked? *Thousands of kids*. So *thousands of kids* is the complete subject of the sentence. And what is the predicate? *Throughout the history of the school . . . have walked these halls.*

Now take a look at this one.

> **There are a million reasons to eat candy.**

First, remember that *there* is never the subject of a sentence; if you see *there* at the beginning, the subject will probably follow the verb. So what is the verb? *Are.* There are *a million reasons*. *A million reasons* is the subject. Therefore, *There are . . . to eat candy* is the predicate.

Underline the complete subject and put parentheses around the complete predicate in each of the following sentences. Check your answers at the back of the book.

Ares wanted this Greek named Odysseus for the army. Should a powerful god of war have to do this work for himself? In the early morning Ares appeared in a dream to the Greek general Menelaus.

"You should go to the island of Ithaca."

"Why should I go there? I like Sparta." Menelaus had a lot on his mind.

"You must find Odysseus and sign him up for the war. I command it."

The Greek general knew he had no choice. He did hope to get some personal benefits out of this trip. "I need new horses and a chariot for the trip. My old chariot is getting very rusty. Can I have a matched pair of black horses?" Menelaus knew how to bargain, even with a god.

"Two black horses and a new chariot are on their way to you. I don't want any more excuses. This trip to Ithaca will be a long one. Start on your way."

"Your slightest wish is my command. I will find Odysseus."

SUBJECT AND PREDICATE REVIEW

Every sentence has a subject and a predicate.

To find the subject, locate the verb. Ask yourself, "Who or what is the verb talking about?" That "who or what" is the subject.

The predicate is the verb and all words related to that verb. The predicate may be a simple verb or a verb phrase. It may also be the verb and all the other phrases that are talking about the subject.

QUIZ #12: COMPLETE SENTENCES

Mark the complete sentences with an "S." Mark the fragments with an "F." Check your answers at the back of the book.

_____ 1. Menelaus did go to Ithaca.

_____ 2. Where he found Odysseus.

_____ 3. Plowing his field with salt and pretending he was insane.

_____ 4. Odysseus was happy with his wife and young child.

_____ 5. And didn't want to go off to war.

_____ 6. Menelaus had to plan a trick.

_____ 7. Which he did, as soon as he thought of a good one.

_____ 8. It's hard to trick a tricky man like Odysseus!

_____ 9. Has history recorded Menelaus's actions?

_____ 10. A trick involving Odysseus's baby son Telemachus.

PHRASES

There are two more terms you need to know before moving on to the more complicated points of grammar. The terms are _phrases_ and _clauses_.

A _phrase_ is a group of words that cannot stand alone as a sentence. The words in a phrase work together as a part of speech. For example, they may work together to name a person, place, thing, or idea. In this case, the group of words would be called a **noun phrase**. The two most common phrases, however, are the **prepositional phrase** and the **verbal phrase**.

Prepositional Phrases

Remember prepositions? They're those little words that locate a noun in time, space, or direction. As we told you earlier, they always have a mate; they're always part of a phrase. These prepositional phrases always begin with a preposition and end with a noun or pronoun. For example:

around the house
preposition noun

through the door
preposition noun

behind him
preposition pronoun

These are all prepositional phrases. Now you have to decide what part of speech these phrases are acting as by looking at how they work in the sentence.

The black cat was standing behind him.

Go through your steps one by one.

What is the verb? *Was standing.*

What was standing? *The black cat. The black cat* is the subject of the sentence.

What does the prepositional phrase tell you? Where the black cat was standing. *Behind him* is a prepositional phrase that acts as an adverb in this sentence. It describes the verb *was standing*.

Here's one more example of an unusual use of a prepositional phrase.

> Before school **is the best time to take a shower.**

What is the verb? *Is.* When is? *Before school.* In this sentence, the prepositional phrase is the subject of the sentence. Because the subject of a sentence is always a noun, the prepositional phrase here acts as a noun.

Prepositional phrases usually act as adverbs or adjectives. When in doubt, ask yourself what the phrase is telling you in the sentence. When you are picking apart sentences for class or homework, it is usually helpful to put parentheses around prepositional phrases. They always work together and sometimes are distracting when you are trying to locate a subject and verb. For example:

> **One of the boys in the group of a million is going to join us.**

Now that's a long and complicated sentence. But you can gather the prepositional phrases like this.

> **One (of the boys) (in the group) (of a million) is going to join us.**

It may be clearer for you to see the verb (*is going*) and the subject (*One*). If you feel confused, try the following quiz. It will probably clear up the structure of a sentence for you.

William Shakespeare, in his plays, sonnets, and poems made use of about 17,677 different words. Of those, 1,700 were brand new—meaning that Shakespeare coined them. Most of these Shakespeare created words are surprisingly common now: accommodation, amazement, assassination, dwindle, frugal, exposure, courtship, eventful, critic, and auspicious are just a few. Check out Coined by Shakespeare: Words and Meanings First Used by the Bard by Jeffrey McQuain and Stanley Malless for a complete listing of Shakespeare's contributions to the English language!

QUIZ #13: PREPOSITIONAL PHRASES

Find the prepositional phrase or phrases in each sentence. Put parentheses around each one. Check your answers at the back of the book.

1. In Ithaca, Odysseus was plowing the field with a donkey.

2. Plowing should be done with oxen, so using donkeys made him look insane.

3. Also, farmers in their right minds plant seeds.

4. Odysseus was planting salt in his fields.

5. But Menelaus set the baby Telemachus in the path of Odysseus's plow.

6. The loving father instantly swerved the plow away from his son.

7. To Menelaus, this action proved he was not a raving madman.

8. Odysseus was now headed for the Trojan War and would not see his son for twenty years.

VERBAL PHRASES

Verbal phrases look like verbs. They contain a word that's something like a verb, and yet the phrase as a whole acts as a noun, an adjective, or an adverb. You'll learn more about this interesting blend on pages 120–125, but here's one example.

Collecting miniature soldiers **can be interesting.**

The verbal phrase, in italics, is used as the subject of the sentence.

CLAUSES

A clause is a group of words that includes a subject and a verb. There are two types of clauses: dependent and independent. An **independent clause**, which is also called a **principal clause**, makes sense standing alone. A dependent clause (also called a **subordinate clause**) is used as a noun, an adjective, or an adverb. It depends on the other clause in the sentence to make sense.

Billy told us that he would come to the party.

This is a sentence that is made up of two separate clauses.

(Billy told us) (that he would come to the party.)
clause 1   clause 2

Both of these clauses have subjects and verbs. But the first clause, *Billy told us*, is the independent, or principal, clause in the sentence. *That he would come to the party* is the dependent clause. It wouldn't make sense by itself, and the words work together as the direct object of the verb *told* in the independent clause. Billy told us what? *That he would come to the party.*

Another example of a **noun clause**, this one used as a subject, is in the sentence below.

That Romeo likes Juliet is obvious.

Something is obvious. We could have had a one-word noun like *truth*. *The truth is obvious.* But instead we had an entire dependent clause fill the slot for the subject: *That Romeo likes Juliet* is a dependent clause with its own subject, verb, and direct object. The entire dependent clause is the subject of *is obvious.*

Dependent clauses can also be used as adjectives or as adverbs. Here is an example of each kind.

Romeo loves the girl whom he met in Verona.

The main clause is *Romeo loves the girl.* Then the dependent clause answers the question "Which girl?" *The girl whom he met in Verona.* Those last five words are an example of an **adjective clause.**

Now for an **adverb clause.**

> When Romeo speaks beautiful poetry to Juliet, he is expressing his love.

The independent clause is *he is expressing his love.* When does he express his love? The dependent clause answers that question: *When Romeo speaks beautiful poetry to Juliet.* Like a one-word adverb, this entire clause answers the question "When?"

(You'll learn more about noun, adjective, and adverb clauses on 201–204 in the chapter on diagramming sentences.)

QUIZ #14: PHRASES AND CLAUSES

Each of the following sentences contains one or two clauses. Underline the dependent clauses and put parentheses around the independent clauses. Check your answers at the back of the book.

1. During the Trojan War, Odysseus showed his own trickiness.

2. Unless you have read Homer's poetry, you may not know about his biggest trick.

3. He dreamed up the idea of the giant artificial horse where soldiers could hide.

4. Before they realized the trick, the Trojans had pulled the beautiful Trojan Horse inside their city walls.

5. They were horrified when, during the dark night, several soldiers crawled out of the belly of the horse!

PHRASES AND CLAUSES REVIEW

A **phrase** is a group of words that does not have a subject and a verb.

The words in a phrase work together as a part of speech.

A **prepositional phrase** always begins with a preposition and ends with a noun or pronoun.

A **clause** is a group of words with a subject and a verb.

A **dependent clause** cannot stand alone as a sentence. It can be used in a sentence as a noun, an adjective, or an adverb.

An **independent clause** makes sense by itself, i.e., a sentence.

SIMPLE, COMPOUND, AND COMPLEX SENTENCES

Some sentences are long and complicated, while others are short and simple. When you first learned to write, you probably wrote in short sentences. But that kind of writing gets boring after a while. Look at this paragraph.

> We went to the game. We sat in the sun. It was hot. We ate hot dogs. They were delicious.

Compare it to this one.

> We went to the game. We sat in the sun, and it was hot. The hot dogs we ate were delicious.

As you can see, you want to mix up your writing by including some compound and complex sentences.

SIMPLE SENTENCES

A **simple sentence** is made up of one clause. It can have more than one noun in the subject, or more than one word in the predicate, and still be simple.

Apples are my favorite.
Apple and cherry are my favorite pies.
Apples make delicious cider or pie.
I like eating dishes made from apples.

In all of these examples, you cannot separate the sentences into two or more clauses.

COMPOUND SENTENCES

A **compound sentence** is made up of two or more independent clauses (or simple sentences) that are joined together with a conjunction. For example:

We hiked to the picnic grounds, and we ate our lunches.
The movie was wonderful, and I would see it again.
Zippy would eat fruit, but he hated vegetables.
Would you like to eat vegetables, or would you rather have candy?

To decide if a sentence is compound, try to divide it into two or more complete sentences. If you can, then the sentence is compound.

COMPLEX SENTENCES

A **complex sentence** has at least one independent clause and at least one dependent clause. You could break the sentence apart, and each part would have a subject and a verb, but at least one of the parts wouldn't make sense alone.

> **Iggy went to the store** where he bought Jujy-fruits.
> **He was convinced** that Jujyfruits were as good as real fruit.

As you can see, the clauses in regular type could stand alone as sentences. The italicized clauses could not.

You may have noticed that a series of simple sentences can be turned into compound or complex sentences, depending on how you connect them. By the same token, if your compound or complex sentences begin to get too compound or complex, it may be easier to break them into smaller, simpler sentences. Sometimes, you can take a long dependent clause and turn it into a simple adjective.

> **Martha lives in a house,** which is made of bricks.
> **Martha lives in a brick house.**

Both of these sentences are correct, but the second one certainly sounds better. Some sentences sound better when they are long and interesting, and some sound better when they are short and simple. Mix them up. Be creative. Reread your sentences to make sure they sound correct and interesting. Work on developing your "ear" for good grammar and good style.

QUIZ #15: COMPOUND AND COMPLEX SENTENCES

Rewrite each of these pairs of simple sentences as one compound or one complex sentence. (There is more than one correct way to rewrite each.) Check your answers at the back of the book.

1. The soldiers came out of the horse. The Trojans were shocked.

2. The soldiers headed for the palace. They set many fires.

_____

_____

_____

_____

3. The sleepy Trojans wanted to stop them. They weren't organized enough.

_____

_____

_____

_____

4. The soldiers got to the palace. It was located at the top of the hill.

_____

_____

_____

_____

5. Priam, the king of Troy, tried to defend himself. He was too old.

_____

_____

_____

_____

6. Priam died bravely. Later, his brave son Hector had to face the fiercest Greek soldier, Achilles.

_____

_____

_____

_____

7. We know Hector was also a family man. He loved his wife, Andromache, and their baby son.

_____

_____

_____

_____

8. Hector's son was frightened by the plume on his father's helmet. Hector removed the helmet.

_____

_____

_____

_____

Rewrite each wordy complex sentences as a simple sentence.

9. The Trojan War began when a prince from Troy whose name was Paris took Helen away from Sparta.

_____

_____

_____

_____

10. You may find it odd that Helen, who was from Greece, is now called Helen of Troy.

_____

_____

_____

_____

SENTENCE REVIEW

A **simple sentence** has one independent clause—a subject and a verb.

A **compound sentence** has two or more independent clauses joined together with a conjunction. If you take it apart, the two clauses will make sense as separate sentences.

A **complex sentence** has at least one independent clause and at least one dependent clause. That dependent clause may be used as a noun, an adjective, or an adverb.

QUIZ #16: PUTTING IT ALL TOGETHER

In the following sentences, circle the verbs of the main clauses and underline the simple subjects. Also, write "S" if it is a simple sentence, "C" if it is a compound sentence, and "X" if it is a complex sentence. Check your answers at the back of the book.

____ 1. Hector had to face Achilles, who was the fiercest of the Greeks.

____ 2. He needed help!

____ 3. But no help was powerful enough to save him from the fierce Achilles.

___ 4. Achilles was especially savage at this time because his best friend had been killed in the war.

___ 5. Although his friend had worn Achilles's armor, he had still been killed.

___ 6. Achilles thirsted for revenge, and Hector was there at just the wrong moment.

___ 7. What a sad event their hand-to-hand battle was!

___ 8. Later, Priam humbly went to see Achilles, and he was able to take his son's body home for a proper funeral.

___ 9. Hector's funeral rites lasted for several days because he had been such an important Trojan warrior.

ONE LAST NOTE . . .

Okay, you've gotten through the first third of the book, the part that is primarily devoted to abstract knowledge. In the next two sections, you'll get some more in-your-head knowledge, but you'll also be moving on to more practical matters of usage. Still, you're going to hear a lot more terms, and some may be confusing at first. Just remember the basics, and never hesitate to turn back and review something. All the terms you've learned are also in the glossary in the back of the book, so remember that you can check there as well.

PART 2

More Knowledge: Abstract and Practical

CHAPTER 3

More About Nouns and Pronouns

In Chapters 1 and 2 of this book, we reviewed each of the basic parts of speech and the main parts and types of sentences. There's a lot more to know about each of these things. In Chapters 3, 4, and 5, we will focus on each of the parts of speech in detail and give you some extra grammar tips.

This chapter is devoted to different types of nouns and all of the rules that come with using them. As you may know, teachers can ask about strange-sounding terms like "collective nouns" and "reflexive pronouns." Don't let the names of these things put you off. We're going to explain them here, too, so you will know what they are.

As you practice grammar and develop your "ear," you will find that you use many of these things naturally in your speech. Speaking and writing properly takes practice. Work on one or two things at a time so you can master each one.

Conjunctions Mnemonic

Here is an easy way to remember some of the most commonly-used conjunctions:

For
And
Nor
But
Or
Yet
So

Use these coordinating conjunctions to join the two parts of a compound sentence.

TYPES OF NOUNS

You know that a noun is a person, place, thing, or idea, right? Now, you can change a noun to mean different things. For example, you can show that there is more than one thing by making the noun plural. Or you can show that a noun "owns" something by making it possessive.

Singular and Plural Nouns

If you have one of something, you use a **singular** noun to refer to it. If you have two or more of those things, you use the **plural** form of the noun.

> If you build a second *house*, you have two *houses*.
> If you find a second *mouse*, you don't have two *mouses*!

Instead, you have two *mice*. Your life would be so much easier if you had simple grammar rules to follow. There are some pretty consistent rules you can follow to show the plural of a word, but there will always be exceptions, and we'll try to cover as many of them as possible. But first, let's go over the rules.

You can make most words plural just by adding an -*s* at the end. For example:

alien/aliens   helicopter/helicopters
pizza/pizzas   book/books
joy/joys   soda/sodas
day/days   pickle/pickles
word/words

If a word ends in -*s*, -*x*, -*z*, -*sh*, or -*ch*, then you must add -*es*.

Why? Because it sounds better. Those words need a different plural ending, or the plural would just run into the word. For example, we say *box-es* not *boxs*. Add the *-es* ending when you hear yourself adding a whole new syllable at the end.

box/boxes	Jones/Joneses
tax/taxes	dress/dresses
lunch/lunches	waltz/waltzes
fox/foxes	mess/messes
wish/wishes	

If a word ends in *f* or *fe*, change the ending to a *v* then add *-es*. Why? Well, it also just sounds better. And, lucky you, it's another rule to remember.

calf/calves	knife/knives
loaf/loaves	elf/elves
leaf/leaves	shelf/shelves
half/halves	life/lives
thief/thieves	

For words that end in *y*, change the *y* to *i* and add *-es* if the *y* comes after a consonant. If the *y* comes after a vowel, just add *s*.

baby/babies	lady/ladies
penny/pennies	monkey/monkeys
toy/toys	story/stories

And then there are the weird ones. Sometimes there are no rules! Some nouns change completely, and some don't change at all when they go from singular to plural. What do you do? If you are ever unsure about a plural noun, look it up. In the dictionary, any unusual plurals are listed right after the singular form of the word. Here are a few.

child/children   moose/moose
sheep/sheep   deer/deer
mouse/mice   woman/women
foot/feet   person/people
tooth/teeth

QUIZ #17: SINGULAR AND PLURAL NOUNS

Change the singular nouns in parentheses to plural nouns. Check your answers at the back of the book.

1. The Greek warriors never ate (banana).

_____

_____

2. Did King Agamemnon have any pet (monkey).

_____

_____

3. No, his throne was flanked by two
   (cheetah) _____,
   whose (foot) _____ had
   extra-long (claw) _____

   _____.

4. He had special (box) _____
   _____ made for these (creature)
   _____ whose
   (name) _____ were
   Agatha and Pantho.

5. Each box had two (shelf) _____
   _____ to hold the spare (collar)
   _____ of the beasts.

6. (Workman) _____
   used (knife) _____ made
   of volcanic lava to craft the scalloped
   (edge) _____ of
   each box.

7. The bronze for the (box) _____
   _____ had to be heated to very
   high (temperature) _____

   _____.

8. You would never see (deer) _____
   _____, (baboon) _____
   _____, or moose sniffing around
   the box.

9. Fine Greek (lady) _____
_____ and (gentleman) _____
_____ also knew to stay away.

10. In fact, all (person) _____
of all social (class) _____
_____ kept their distance when
Agatha and Pantho arrived.

Collective Nouns

A collective noun is a noun that refers to a group of people who usually act together. Because of this collective action, the noun is almost always treated as singular. If there is more than one group of people, the noun is plural. Some examples of collective nouns are *audience, jury, family, government,* and *class.* Look at the following sentences.

> The seventh-grade class went to Washington, D.C.
> *(The noun is singular because it refers to one group that is acting together.)*
> The seventh- and eighth-grade classes went to the museum.
> *(The noun is plural because it refers to two groups acting together.)*

Possessive Form of Nouns (that take on the function of an adjective)

If a person, place, or thing "owns" something, you can use a **possessive noun.** (In this possessive form, many teachers and grammar books will ask you to classify the word as an adjective.) This possessive form will make your sentences sound much smoother and clearer. For example, instead of

the coat of *Bert*
the sweater of *Ernie*
a vacation of a *week*

you can say

Bert's coat
Ernie's sweater
a *week's* vacation

As you know, a noun is either singular or plural. That will affect how you make it into a possessive.

If a noun is singular, always add -'s, even if it ends in *s*. For example:

Bert	Bert's hat
Charles	Charles's homework
dress	dress's hemline
girl	girl's house
James	James's bicycle

Okay, we admit that *James's* looks a little odd. And, to be honest, if you wrote *James'* that would be okay, too. But to be safe and to keep your rules as simple as possible, remember that all singular nouns get -'s at the end when made possessive.

If a noun is plural but doesn't end in *s*, add -'s. If it does end in *s*, just add the apostrophe. Let's take a look.

babies	babies' room
children	children's room
ladies	ladies' room
men	men's room

To summarize, just add -'s to any noun to show that it is possessive unless it is a plural noun ending in *s*. Then, simply add the apostrophe.

Fill in the missing parts of the following chart. Check your answers at the back of the book.

Singular	Singular Possessive	Plural	Plural Possessive
berry cat			
desk dog			
family glove			
house Jones			
peach thief			

Direct And Indirect Objects

Remember that to find the subject of a sentence, ask yourself what the verb is, and then what is performing that action. That's the subject. The **direct object** of the sentence is the receiver of the action. Let's start with a simple sentence.

> Bozo threw confetti.

What's the verb? *Threw.* Who threw? *Bozo. Bozo* is the subject of the sentence. He does the throwing. What is getting thrown? *Confetti.* So, *confetti* is the direct object of the sentence.

You must have a direct object before you can have an **indirect object**. If we give you more information about this event (Bozo threw the audience confetti), *the audience* is the indirect object. It tells you "to whom" or "for whom" the action is being done. You can always spot an indirect object by pulling it out and making into a prepositional phrase. In this case, you may have said

> Bozo threw confetti (at the audience).

Look at this one.

> Zelda gave Zorba a fancy jacket.

Zelda is the subject. What is the direct object and the indirect object of the verb *gave*? What did she give? *A fancy jacket*. That is the direct object. *Zorba* is the indirect object. You can check by making it into a prepositional phrase.

Zelda gave a fancy jacket (to Zorba).

It is also worth remembering that if you have both a direct object and an indirect object, the indirect object usually comes between the verb and the direct object.

QUIZ #19: FINDING DIRECT AND INDIRECT OBJECTS

In each of the following sentences, circle the direct object and underline the indirect object (if one exists). Check your answers at the back of the book.

1. Zeus gave Hera her birthday present.

2. Hera thanked him over and over.

3. The special mirror gave her a real thrill.

4. She also showed her personal attendant this handmade looking glass.

5. Her servant admired it greatly.

Predicate Nouns (sometimes called predicate nominatives)

One kind of noun you find in the predicate of a sentence is an object (direct or indirect.) But some verbs do not take objects. The most common example is the verb *to be (is, are, will, am,* etc.*).* The verb *to be* is like an equals sign. In this case, the noun in the predicate will rename or explain the subject. Other verbs that may take predicate nouns or pronouns instead of direct objects are *to become, to seem,* and *to appear.* You can always tell a predicate noun or pronoun because it will be equal to the subject. If you're pointing at it, you're pointing at the subject.

> *Krusty is my favorite clown.*
> (Krusty = clown, so *clown* is the predicate noun.)
>
> *Homer Simpson is a strange father.*
> (Homer Simpson = father, so *father* is the predicate noun.)
>
> *Springfield is the largest city in the state.*
> (Springfield = city, so city is the predicate noun.)

Not all sentences have predicate nouns. To determine whether a noun is a predicate noun or a direct object, just ask yourself if it equals the subject.

Lisa plays the saxophone.
(Lisa = saxophone? No, so *saxophone* is th[e]
direct object.)

Lisa is the lead in the play.
(Lisa = lead? Yes, so *lead* is the predicat[e]
noun.)

**Underline the predicate nouns in the fol-
lowing sentences. Check your answers at the
back of the book.**

1. Cupid was the god of love.

2. Hercules was the strongest resident of
   Olympus.

3. The god of the hearth was Hestia.

4. She appears as the subject of very few
   stories.

5. The hearth was the spot where she
   remained.

TYPES OF PRONOUNS

Remember that a pronoun takes the place of a noun.

Personal Pronouns

Personal pronouns take on different forms depending on to whom they refer.

First person refers to the speaker: *I, me, mine, my, we, us, our,* and *ours* are all the pronouns you would use if you were speaking in the first person (the speaker is talking about himself or herself).

Second person refers to the person being spoken to: *you, your,* and *yours* are pronouns. You would use them if you were speaking directly to someone.

Third person refers to the person being spoken about: *he, him, his, she, her, hers, it, its, they, them, their,* and *theirs* are pronouns you would use if you were talking about other people.

Formal Reports

Some teachers may ask you not to use the second person, *you,* in your written work, unless you're referring to one specific individual. The pronoun *one,* however, can sound overly formal and awkward. What's a student to do? Often, you can find a graceful way around the problem. For example, you can avoid the "phoney" sound of this sentence:

> One will see this insect species I have described in the picture below.

by saying simply

> The insect species I have described is pictured below.

Pronoun Case

There are two sets of personal pronouns—subject pronouns and object pronouns. *Subject* pronouns are sometimes referred to as being in the **nominative case**. *Object* pronouns are referred to as being in the **objective case**.

Nominative (Subject) Pronouns

Singular	Plural
I	we
you	you
he, she, it	they

You can use a subject pronoun as:

1. The subject of a sentence. The subject is the doer of he action described by the verb.

   She threw the ball. (Who threw? *She*)
   I went to the party. (Who went? *I*)
   We wanted ice cream. (Who wanted? *We*)
   They came to our store. (Who came? *They*)

2. After using a form of the verb *to be* (*am, is, are*, or *will*, for example). Remember, the verb *to be* is like an equals sign; anything after it will be in the same form as is before it. If you have a subject noun before, you need a subject pronoun after. You can think of this as the "phone rule." It's the way you answer the phone—when someone calls and says, "I'm looking for a Ms. Oakley," the person would answer, "This is she." But if Ms. Oakley found that too stilted, she could say, "I'm Ms. Oakley."

Objective (Object) Pronouns

Singular	Plural
me	us
you	you
him, her, it	them

You can use an object pronoun as:

1. The direct object of a verb. The subject of a verb is the doer of the action. The direct object of the verb is the receiver of the action.

> She asked *me* to come to the party. (Whom did she ask? *Me*.)
> I picked *them*. (I picked what? *Them*.)

2. As the indirect object of a verb. An indirect object tells to whom or for whom the action is being done.

> I picked *her* flowers.
> Marilyn gave *him* a punch on the nose.

3. As the object of a preposition.

> I gave the flowers to *her*.
> We ran with *them* to the race.

Some Tips

One of the most common errors people make is to confuse the subject and object pronouns. There are a few common pitfalls that, with practice, you can avoid.

1. Say *between you and me...*, not *between you and I*. The pronouns are the objects of the preposition *between* and are always in objective form. The correct use

is *between you and him,* or *between me and him,* or whatever pronouns you use.

2. If you are making a comparison, complete the comparison in your head to decide if you need a subject or object pronoun.

> **Sally is smarter than *I / me*.**

Finish the comparison:

> **Sally is smarter than *I am*.**
>
> **She is as tall as *he / him*.**

Finish the comparison:

> **She is as tall as *he is*.**

This rule may seem a little strange, so you should practice it.

3. If you have a compound subject or predicate, try saying each one separately to figure it out.

> **Bob and *I / me* went to the store.**

To check:

> **Bob went to the store.**
> ***I* went to the store.**

Now try this one:

> Mary went with Paul and *him / he*.

To check:

> Mary went with Paul.
> Mary went with *him*.

What about:

> *We / Us* kids went on the hike last Saturday.

To check:

> Take out *kids*: We went on the hike last Saturday, so *we* is correct.

For more practice on the correct form of pronouns, see pages 141–146 in Chapter 6 on Common Mistakes.

QUIZ #21: SUBJECT AND OBJECT PRONOUNS

Underline the correct pronoun in each of the following sentences. Check your answers at the back of the book.

Mr. Epstein's Favorite Gods

One day, when the sixth grade class was studying mythology, the students looked up at their teacher, Mr. Epstein. (They, Them) wanted to know what (he, him) thought of the Greek gods.

Jeff said, "Mr. Epstein, believe (I, me), we're not trying to get out of writing our in-class report. But please tell (we, us) which god is your favorite."

"Well, Jeff," replied Mr. Epstein, "let (I, me) think a minute. I don't like war, so I won't pick Ares or anyone like (he, him). Since my hobby is scuba diving, (I, me) am going to go with Poseidon, god of the sea."

"And your favorite goddess?" asked Stephanie. "(We, Us) kids are thinking you'll pick Athena because (she, her) is wise like you."

"Just between you and (I, me)," laughed Mr. Epstein, "I think men and women who handle love well are the wisest of all. Let (I, me) vote for Aphrodite."

"Terrific," said Stephanie. "I'll make a poster with drawings of both of (they, them) on it! Where are my Magic Markers?"

Possessive Pronouns

You know that you need to add -'s to make a noun possessive. But with pronouns, it's a different story. Possessive pronouns do not take apostrophes at all. Take a look at the personal pronouns and their possessive forms. (Many grammar books and teachers treat possessive pronouns as adjectives when they are in a sentence such as "My book is in my locker." Which book? Which locker? *My* is working as an adjective.)

Personal pronoun	Possessive form
I, me	my
you	your
he, him	his
she, her	hers
we, us	ours
they, them	theirs
it	its
who, whom	whose

There is no apostrophe in the possessive form of these pronouns. Don't confuse the possessive forms of some pronouns with similar contractions.

its (possessive form)   *it's* (contraction standing for *it is*)

whose (possessive form)   *who's* (contraction standing for *who is*)

Relative, Reflexive, Demonstrative, and Interrogative Pronouns

Okay, don't panic. These are actually pretty easy. Let's look at them one at a time.

Relative Pronouns

These pronouns link a relative clause to the main clause of a sentence. There are two types of relative pronouns: definite and indefinite. Definite relative **pronouns** stand for a definite noun. **Indefinite relative pronouns** are not preceded by a definite noun (also called an antecedent).

Definite Relative Pronouns	Indefinite Relative Pronouns
which	what
that	which
who	whoever
whom	whatever
	whom
	whomever

> Zelda went to see F. Scott, *who* was quite dashing in his white suit.

The main clause of this sentence is *Zelda went to see F. Scott. Who was quite dashing in his white suit* is a relative clause because it cannot stand alone. Here it modifies, or describes, *F. Scott*. The relative pronoun *who* links the two clauses.

The following are the rules for relative pronouns:

1. If you are deciding between **who** and **whom**, just substitute *he* and *him*. If you would use *he*, then use *who*. If you would use *him*, then use *whom*.

2. **Who** and **whom** refer to people.

3. **That** can refer to people, animals, or things.

4. **Which** cannot refer to people.

5. **That** and **which** are often used interchangeably by very good writers, but some very careful users of the language will ask you to make a distinction. In general, *that* begins an adjective clause that is essential to the meaning of a sentence. *Which* introduces an adjective clause that is nonessential to the meaning of the sentence. *Which* generally follows a comma; *that* doesn't.

> I like apples *that* are green and tart. (The adjective clause is essential to the meaning of the sentence. Sometimes these clauses are called restrictive because they limit the meaning of the word they describe.)

> I like apples, *which* are very healthy and good to eat. (The adjective clause is not essential to the sentence's meaning. It simply adds addi-

tional information. Sometimes these clauses are called nonrestrictive because they do not limit the meaning of the word they describe.)

Alligators *that* are pink are nonexistent. (Alligators do exist, so the adjective clause is essential to the meaning of the sentence.)

Alligators, *which* are grayish-green, may be seen in Florida. (In general, alligators are grayish-green, so the adjective clause is not essential to the meaning of the sentence.)

QUIZ #22: RELATIVE PRONOUNS

Underline the correct relative pronoun in each of the following sentences. Check your answers at the back of the book.

1. Athens, (which, that) is the main city in Greece, is named for Athena.

2. Athena, (who, whom) was the goddess of wisdom, often had an owl with her.

3. Owls (which, that) lived in the Temple of Athena were very fortunate.

4. Athena was the goddess for (who, whom) a large statue was made.

5. (Who, Whom) has seen a picture of the building called the Parthenon?

Reflexive Pronouns

When you think of reflexive pronouns, think about reflections. These pronouns act like mirrors. They refer to the subject in the sentence. The reflexive pronouns are *myself, yourself, herself, himself, ourselves, yourselves, themselves,* and *itself.* Check out the following rules:

1. Make sure that the reflexive pronoun agrees with the noun it mirrors.

    > They went around talking about *themselves.*
    > David ate all 50 cookies by *himself.*

2. You may use them for emphasis, but don't do it too often.

    > She won the championship *herself.*
    > I, *myself,* am quite proud of my accomplishment.

3. Don't substitute reflexive pronouns for subject pronouns.

    > Paul and *I* went to the museum.
    > not
    > Paul and *myself* went to the museum.

Demonstrative Pronouns

A demonstrative pronoun demonstrates the noun in the sentence that is being talked about. The demonstrative pronouns are *that, these, this,* and *those.* Here are the rules.

1. A demonstrative pronoun must take the place of a specific noun. Otherwise, it is really just an adjective.

   > I want to drink all of *this.* (*This* refers to something the speaker is pointing to, such as milk or apple juice, so it is a demonstrative pronoun.)

   > *This* dress is new. (*This* is an adjective describing the dress. Which dress? This dress.)

   > *Those* are completely worthless! (*Those* refers to things the speaker is talking about, so it is a demonstrative pronoun.)

   > *Those* books are completely worthless! (*Those* is an adjective modifying books. Which books? Those books.)

2. Remember, using demonstrative pronouns is not an excuse for being imprecise. You need to let your reader or listener know what it is you are referring to.

Interrogative Pronouns

As the name suggests, these pronouns are used to interrogate, or ask questions. The interrogative, or question pronouns, are *who, whom, which,* and *what.*

> *Who* are you?
> *What* do you want?
> *Which* house do you live in?
> *Whom* do you want to see?

Pronoun Agreement

Although this is the last pronoun topic we are covering, it is one of the most important. When you use a pronoun, you must be sure that it agrees in number with the noun it replaces: Use a *singular* pronoun to replace a singular noun. Use a *plural* pronoun to replace a plural noun. For example:

> Mr. Joyboy saw *two shells* on the beach and picked *them* up.
> *Siobhan* found *her* green hat lying on the bench.

As with all rules, there are a few points to keep in mind.

The A NOSE Rule

As a rule, use singular pronouns to refer to any of these words: anybody, anything, nobody, nothing, neither, one, someone, something, each, every, and either. You can remember them because they begin with the letters A, N, O, S, or E. For example:

> The teacher felt that *everyone* should do *his* part on the island.
> *Neither* Ferdinand *nor* Sven felt *he* was going to be rescued.

As you can see, this rule may sometimes lead to awkward-sounding sentences. You may end up writing things like:

> Before *a boy or a girl* tries out for sports, *he* should practice.

Technically, that's correct. But realistically it sounds stupid and sexist. What happened to the girl? Should you say:

> Before *a boy or a girl* tries out for sports, *he or she* should practice.

Yikes! You're being even more awkward with that one. How about the following:

> Before *a boy or a girl* tries out for sports, *they* should practice.

We'll be honest—this is how most people handle it. But it's wrong! Sloppy! Don't fall for the *they trap*. *They* has become an all-purpose pronoun used by people who can't dig themselves out of the grammar trap. What to do? When in doubt, rewrite. How about:

> Before *boys and girls* try out for sports, *they* should practice.

By rewriting the whole sentence with a plural subject, you get to use the nice, easy plural pronoun *they.* You haven't offended anyone, and your sentence is grammatically correct. Be consistent.

Remember not to switch pronouns in a sentence.

> *You* must turn on your iPod before listening to *your* music.

not

> *One* must turn on *your* stereo before listening to *one's* music.

Make the nouns that go with your pronouns consistent in number.

> *Each* of the boys asked for *a raise* in *his* allowance.

not

> *Each* of the boys asked for *raises* in *his* allowance. (Individual boys get one raise each.)
> *All* the students took *books* out of the library.

not

> *All* the students took *a book* out of the library. (If there's more than one student, there should be more than one book.

Make sure your reader knows which noun you are referring to when you use a pronoun. Look at the following sentence.

> Will told Sam that he thought *his* report would earn an A.

Is Will being proud of his own work? Or is Will giving his classmate a compliment? Avoid the confusion by rewriting.

> Will wasn't always so self-confident, but *he* told Sam he thought *his* report would earn an A.

or (for the other meaning)

> Will liked Sam's paper and told *him he* thought it would earn an A.

Cross out the incorrect pronoun in each sentence and replace it with a better one. Check your answers at the back of the book.

1. Either Mackenzie or Lana was sure to have brought their new bathing suit.

2. Anybody who have read *The Diary of Anne Frank* know that they have read a classic.

3. "If anyone finds a way out of the maze, would they please let us know?" cried the court jester.

4. "Oh, Brad," said Ms. Gioia, "neither Gaston nor you is able to figure out what they really want."

5. "All of them are happy as clams at high tide to be here. We want to stay at this camp forever," cried Jenna.

CHAPTER 4

More About Verbs

Verbs are the very heart of a sentence. They express action or a state of being. Without a verb, you cannot have a sentence. So, you might say that the verb is the engine of the sentence, the part that makes the sentence work. There's a lot to learn about them, so let's get started.

CHARACTERISTICS OF VERBS

Number: Singular or Plural

You must make sure that the subject and verb agree in number: *Singular* subjects take *singular* verbs. *Plural* subjects take *plural* verbs.

How simple could life be? How do you recognize a singular and a plural verb? Well, in general, you add -*s* to a noun to make it *plural,* and add -*s* to a verb in the *he, she,* or *it* form to make it *singular.* Strange, but true. Check it out.

Singular	Plural
The girl jumps.	The girls jump.
The kitten frolics.	The kittens frolic.
The fat lady sings.	The fat ladies sing.
The shark swims.	The sharks swim.

Of course, this isn't true for all verbs, but it is true for most of them. In general, you must first check the subject; then ask yourself if the subject is singular or plural. Then, make sure the verbs match.

> *Greg and Cindy were* afraid of the ghost that haunted the attic.
> *My sister,* the silly one, *was* sick of figs.

Don't be fooled by a group of words that may separate the subject and the verb. Remember to bracket off the prepositional phrases—they are never part of the subject.

> The *bunch* (of kids) (in the yard) *is* going to sing a song.
> *One* (of the several thousand) (in the state) *was* going to make it to the semifinals.

Subject-Verb Agreement Tips
1. Bracket off prepositional phrases—they are never part of the subject.
2. Locate the verb. Ask yourself who or what is doing the action.
3. Identify the subject.
4. The subject and the verb should match. Plural subjects take plural verbs, and singular subjects take singular verbs.
5. Subjects joined by *and* are plural. Subjects joined by *or* are singular.

Jan *or* Cindy *is* going to win.
Greg *and* Bobby *are* the best swimmers around.

Match the correct verb with the subject in the following sentences. Underline each correct verb. Check your answers at the back of the book.

1. Haley (cook, cooks) for the kids every night.

2. Every night, she (make, makes) their favorite meal: meatloaf.

3. "(Wasn't, Weren't) we going to have something different tonight, Haley?" (ask, asks) Sherman.

4. "Yikes! Meatloaf again!" (cries, cry) Catherine and Emily. "What about us vegetarians?"

5. "(Doesn't, Don't) you people have anything better to do than worry about dinner?"(wonder, wonders) Haley.

6. "Oh, I (am, is) sick of trying to please all of you whiners!" Haley says, as she (pull, pulls) her cookbook out of the drawer once again.

Voice: Active or passive?

You may use two types of voices when you are writing—the active voice and the passive voice. In the **active voice**, the subject is performing the action. In the **passive voice**, the action happens to the subject. For example:

> **Active:** Michael drove the car.
> **Passive:** The car was driven by Michael.

As you can imagine, it is usually preferable to use the active voice when you are writing—it's almost always clearer that way. When you use the passive voice, the sentence often sounds flat or stilted. Here are a few more examples.

> **Active:** We attended the concert.
> **Passive:** The concert was attended by us.
> **Active:** Cats purr to indicate contentment.
> **Passive:** Contentment in cats is indicated by purring.

Tense: Past or Present?

Verbs tell you not only *what* happened, but *when* it happened. The "when" part is called the verb **tense**. There are three main tenses: present, past, and future.

Present Tense

This tense shows that something is happening right now.

> I *am* here.
> Right now, I *am listening* to my best friend.

It can also show something you do all the time.

> Every day at three o'clock, I *run* to the track for practice.
> I *take* a shower every morning.

You should use the present tense when you are stating a fact or an opinion.

Sons of Belial *is* the best band around. Dogs are sometimes called canines.

Past Tense

This tense shows that you are talking or writing about something that has already happened.

> Yesterday, I *fell* down.
> An hour ago, I *went* to the store.
> Once upon a time, a beautiful princess *was born*.

Any time the action takes place in the past, whether it was an hour ago or a thousand years ago, you use the past tense. Most stories are written in the past tense—it is the easiest and most natural way to tell a story—but sometimes the present tense can create a good effect. In the next quiz, try both versions and see what you think.

QUIZ #25: PAST AND PRESENT TENSE OF VERBS

Here is an old story (originally written by the Roman poet Ovid in the first century BCE) told in the present tense. Change all the verbs, as appropriate, to the past tense and compare the effect. Which version do you prefer?

One day in an ancient land, a sculptor named Pygmalion decides to create a statue of a beautiful woman. He buys a large block of the finest Parian marble and brings it to his workshop. Using all his skill, he begins to shape it from an oblong block into the form of a human. Day and night he works, and slowly the cold marble takes on the shape of a woman. Pygmalion can hardly believe his skill has been able to bring forth such beauty.

Strangely enough, he begins to fall in love with the statue. He brings gifts—a bunch of violets, an amber necklace, a broken shell of a robin's egg—and offers to it (or "her," as he is beginning to think of the statue).

"Dear goddess of love," he prays one night, "please grant me this one favor. Can you give life to my creation?"

And as he watches in amazement, the pale white cheeks of the marble image turn pink with life, and the rigid statue starts to bend toward him with a kiss!

(Almost two thousand years later, a British playwright named George Bernard Shaw gives the name *Pygmalion* to his play about a professor of linguistics who transforms a nearly illiterate young woman, Eliza Doolittle, into someone who can be mistaken for a princess. Perhaps you know some songs from the musical version, called *My Fair Lady*?)

Future Tense

This is the tense that is used to show what is going to happen.

> Tomorrow, I *will go* to the banana-eating contest.
> In an hour, I *will run in the race.*
> *Next year, I will be* in high school.

Those three tenses—present, past, and future—are the most common. There are, however, more than three tenses. Before we talk about how the different tenses are formed, we must discuss the principal parts of the verb.

Principal Parts

Three forms of a verb are the most important—they are used to form the different tenses. They are called the principal parts of the verb: the **present tense**, the **past tense**, and the **past participle.**

Regular Verbs

A regular verb is a verb in which the principal parts are all formed the same way—the past tense and past participle are formed by adding *-ed, -d,* or *-t* to the present tense. For example:

Present	Past	Past Participle
ask	asked	asked
climb	climbed	climbed
dive	dived	dived
drag	dragged	dragged
drown	drowned	drowned
sneak	sneaked	sneaked

The Perfect Tenses

Use the **present perfect** if

1. The action started in the past and continues to the present.

> I *have sneaked* two miles so far. (I am still *sneaking*.)

2. The action started in the past and was finished at an earlier time.

> I *have sneaked* 150 miles in my spy-training routine so far.

Use the **past perfect** if

1. You want to show one thing that happened in the past, before something else that happened in the past.

> Before I sneaked to his house, I *had sneaked* to three other houses.

Use the **future perfect** if

1. You want to show an action that will be completed at some future time. (This is a rarely used tense.)

> By next Tuesday, I *will have sneaked* around the whole neighborhood.

◯ **Tip**

Four of the tenses have words that tip you off to them.

Future: *shall* or *will* (You'll see *shall* mostly in writing from an earlier period.)

Present Perfect: *has* or *have*

Past Perfect: *had*

Future perfect: *shall have* or *will have*

Helping Verbs

You may have noticed that many sentences have verbs that are more than one word long. Verbs may be two or three words long, as you can see in the future perfect tense. In the following example, there is a main verb and one or two helping verbs. (Some grammar books call them *auxiliary verbs*.) Taken together, the main verb and the helping verbs are called a **verb phrase**.

He *will have eaten* all my favorite cookies by next week.

Here, *will have* is the helping verb for the main verb, *eaten.*

Fill in the correct verb form in each blank. The verb is in the infinitive form at the end of each sentence. Check your answers at the back of the book.

1. Yesterday, Aloyisius _____ 27 chocolate chip cookies. (to eat)

2. Before he ate the cookies, he _____ four dozen. (to bake)

3. Right now, Spearminta _____ (chew) her favorite chewing gum.

4. Tomorrow, Phileas and Passepartout _____ to Tasmania. (to go)

5. By next Wednesday, Jerome _____ a total of 10 books this summer. (to read)

6. Herman's collection of Popsicle sticks _____ second prize in the world competition. (to win)

7. Dave and Lisa's productivity _____ after they stopped dating. (to drop)

8. Johnny Johnson was sent to jail after he ____ to take over Jimmy's empire. (to threaten)

9. After he had wondered why everyone had giggled at him all day, Beth _____ Matthew that someone had taped the words "kick me" to the back of his sweater. (to tell)

10. Joe _____ crazy gadgets out of duct tape and clay in his spare time. (to build)

IRREGULAR VERBS

Irregular verbs are verbs that do not follow the standard formula for making past tense verbs and past participles. Some irregular verbs are so common that you don't really have to think about them. *To be* is a commonly used irregular verb: I *am*, I *was*, I *have been*, I *will have been*.

Principal Parts of Some Irregular Verbs

Present	Past	Past Participle
blow	blew	blown
bring	brought (not brang)	brought
creep	crept	crept
draw	drew	drawn
drink	drank	drunk
freeze	froze	frozen
get	got	got, gotten
grow	grew	grown
hang	hung	hung (I hung a picture)
	hanged	hanged (They hanged the criminal)
lay	laid	laid (I laid the book down.)
lie	lay	lain (I have lain in bed.)
ring	rang	rung
shake	skook	shaken
shrink	shrank, shrunk	shrunk, shrunken
sink	sank	sunk
slay	slew	slain
spring	sprang, sprung	sprung
swear	swore	sworn
swim	swam	swum

Present	Past	Past Participle
tear	tore	torn
weep	wept	wept
wring	wrung	wrung

Underline the correct tense of the verb in each sentence. Check your answers at the back of the book.

1. Jake (wept, weeped) when he heard the bad news.

2. "My brother has (grew, grown)," he said.

3. "I have (laid, lain) on my bed too long!" she exclaimed.

4. "If I had (tore, torn) that piece of paper, no one would have found out."

5. "I (brang, brought) this on myself," thought Rosa.

6. Mr. Wysiwyg (swore, sworn) that his daughter Phoenicia would never marry an alligator wrestler.

7. Kurt Angle (hanged, hung) his Olympic gold medals on his bedroom wall.

8. Many competitors have (froze, frozen) in fear at the sight of Sackerson.

9. The match began when the timekeeper (rang, rung) the bell.

10. His confidence had been (shaken, shook) when the dodgeball referee ruled his lucky shorts too short.

Lay vs. Lie
Have you ever been corrected for saying that you were so tired, you just wanted to "lay down" in bed? You wouldn't be the first person to confuse the verbs lay and lie.

The verb lay means "to set something down." The verb lie means "to rest, or recline in a horizontal position." You can remember that lay is the more active verb ("lay the book on the table"), while lie is a passive verb ("the books are lying on the table.") And if that doesn't help you remember, next time you're feeling exhausted imagine a cook laying a filet on a tray and a pig lying in a sty under the sun, and then go lie down!

VERBALS

Verbals look like verbs and have some qualities of verbs, but they also act like nouns, adjectives, or adverbs. There are three types: **participles**, **gerunds**, and **infinitives**. Think of verbals as the language equivalent on an amphibian, the animal that is partly a land creature, partly a water creature.

Participles

A participle looks like a verb, but it isn't completely a verb. Think of a participle as a verb that acts like an adjective in a sentence. Look at the difference.

> I *had fallen* down the stairs.
> The leaf, *fallen* from the tree, was quite beautiful.

In the first sentence, *had fallen* is the verb. In the second, the past participle *fallen* is used by itself as an adjective to describe the leaf.

Here are a couple more examples.

> I *had known* that he would be famous one day.
> *Known* for his great laugh, Billy was famous.

In the first sentence, *had known* is the main verb in the sentence. In the second sentence, *known* is used to help describe Billy; it is a participle, a verb form used as an adjective.

A participle may be part of a phrase. You have to be sure that the phrase is placed close to the word it modifies. For example:

> Waiting for his call, the phone just wouldn't ring!

This sentence contains an error. The structure of the sentence makes it sound as if the participial phrase *waiting for his call* is something the phone was doing. A correct version would be like this: *Waiting for his call, Georgia thought the phone would never ring.* "Waiting for his call" modifies "Georgia." She's the one doing the waiting.

See more on this frequent error in Chapter 6.

Put parentheses around the participles in the following sentences. Check your answers at the back of the book.

1. When he discovered his missing barbecued ribs, Vince called for Linda.

2. Christian used the peaches picked from the tree to bake a pie.

3. Mr. Austin thought that Sean's answer was wrong because it included a misspelled word.

4. It is a great convenience to have running water.

5. There were so many screaming children in the movie.

Gerunds

Participles are verbals that are used as adjectives, but gerunds are verbals that are used as nouns. Gerunds are easy to spot: They are verb forms ending in *–ing*, but they serve the function of a noun in the sentence. For example:

Skating is my favorite thing to do.

Skating is used as a noun here; it acts as the subject of the sentence.

Here's another example.

Collecting stamps is Edwina's favorite hobby.

Collecting is not completely a verb in this sentence; it is a verb form used as a gerund. The phrase *Collecting stamps* is the subject of the verb *is*. But things get trickier here! *Collecting* retains enough of its verb function to take its own direct object, *stamps*. Remember that "amphibian" nature of verbals: They're neither this nor that—but both!

QUIZ #29: GERUNDS

Underline the gerund in each of the following sentences. Check your answers at the back of the book.

1. I always liked playing baseball.

2. We all enjoyed running out onto the field.

3. Batting is the one thing I don't do well.

4. Fielding is my area of expertise.

5. Winning tournaments, however, is something everybody likes.

Infinitives

Infinitives are verbals that can act as nouns, adjectives, or adverbs. An infinitive is a verb form preceded by the word *to*. If you see *to* with a noun or pronoun, it's a prepositional phrase, but if you see *to* with a verb, it's an infinitive. The infinitives of the verb *help,* for example, are *to help, to have helped, to be helped,* and *to have been helped.*

> **Noun:** Doctors hope *to help* their patients.
> **Adjective:** Which of these books would be the one *to help* me study? (*To help* modifies the pronoun one.)
> **Adverb:** My sister told us stories *to help* pass the time. (*To help* modifies the verb *told.*)

QUIZ #30: INFINITIVES

Underline the infinitive in each of the following sentences. Check your answers at the back of the book.

1. Michiko wanted to see the sights in Dallas.

2. To go to the races was Nathan's favorite pastime.

3. Mr. Settepane wanted to dine at his competitor's restaurant.

4. Valerie hoped to win the track meet that week.

5. Jerry always has to run from Tom after school.

6. Ralph waits until the teacher is out of the room before he starts to eat his shoelaces.

7. "To work at the DMV is no picnic," Arlene said to Max.

CHAPTER 5
More About Modifiers

ADJECTIVES AND ADVERBS

What Are the Comparative Forms?

Using the right adjective is easy if you know the rules. Most adjectives have three forms: the positive, the comparative, and the superlative. Use the **positive form** when you are talking about one thing, the **comparative form** when you are comparing two things, and the **superlative form** when you are comparing more than two things.

> **Positive:** The berry is *sweet.*
> **Comparative:** The blueberry is *sweeter* than the strawberry. (comparing two things)
> **Superlative:** The raspberry is the *sweetest* berry of all. (comparing more than two things)

The Comparative and the Superlative

If an adjective has only *one* syllable, add *-er* for the comparative form and *-est* for the superlative form. If the last letter is *-y,* change the *y* to an *i.*

Positive	Comparative	Superlative
slow	slower	slowest
fast	faster	fastest
dry	drier	driest

When an adjective has *two* syllables, things get a little trickier. Sometimes, you will add *-er* for the comparative form and *-est* for the superlative form. At other times, you will add *more* for the comparative form and *most* for the superlative form. If you are not sure, check the dictionary. It will suggest which comparative and superlative forms to use.

Positive	Comparative	Superlative
silly	sillier	silliest
funny	funnier	funniest
graceful	more graceful	most graceful

If an adjective has three or more syllables, add *more* for the comparative form and *most* for the superlative form.

Positive	Comparative	Superlative
ridiculous	more ridiculous	most ridiculous
argumentative	more argumentative	most argumentative

Some common adjectives have irregular comparative and superlative forms. Check out the following examples.

Positive	Comparative	Superlative
bad	worse	worst
good	better	best
little	less	least
many	more	most

For example:

> **Positive:** Joan is *friendly*.
> **Comparative:** Peter is *less friendly* than Joan.
> **Superlative:** Nancy is the *least friendly* of anyone in the class.

However, some adjectives never take a comparative or superlative form because they express something that is perfect or complete. In other words, they cannot be more or less. For example:

unique
perfect
infinite
dead

Something cannot be more unique or less perfect. If you really need to modify these adjectives, you should use adverbs, such as nearly, almost, or hardly, to show that something approaches these qualities.

> nearly perfect
> almost dead
> hardly unique

Finally, you should always avoid using double comparisons such as *more uglier* or *most friendliest.* Use either *uglier* or *friendliest* instead.

QUIZ #31: COMPARATIVE FORMS OF ADJECTIVES

Underline the correct adjective form in the following sentences. Check your answers at the back of the book.

1. Of all the kids, Vernon was the (smarter, smartest).

2. Taylor was (quieter, quietest) than Jennifer.

3. Of the various popular snack foods, Harold likes pizza (better, best).

4. Nell and Cynthia are both odd, but Cynthia is the (odder, oddest).

5. Pierre is the (more, most) mysterious person I have ever met.

Using the Correct Adverb/Adjective

Adverbs and adjectives are commonly confused, because they often sound very similar. If you are unsure if a word is an adverb or an adjective, look it up. Keep in mind that many adverbs end in -*ly*. But—most important—remember that adverbs modify verbs, adjectives, and other adverbs, while adjectives modify nouns or pronouns. Look at the following sentences.

> Cindy went *quick/quickly* up the stairs. (Use *quickly*, the adverb, because you are describing a verb, *went.*)
> She is a *quick/quickly* runner. (Use *quick* because you are describing a noun, *runner.*)

The Good/Well Confusion

Good and *well* are words that everybody mixes up. How often have you heard, "I just know you'll do good on that test"? That's wrong. Remember that *good* is an adjective and *well* is an adverb. If you are talking about how you will "do," then you need to modify it with an adverb. Check out the following examples.

> That song is *good.* You play it *well.*
> This meatloaf is *good.* You cook so *well.*

Well can also be an adjective. It may convey a different shade of meaning from *good*. So, it is correct to say:

> You look *well*. (you don't look sick) OR You look good in red. (you're attractive in red)
> I feel *well*. (I was sick last week) OR I feel good. (I'm happy, in general good shape)

QUIZ #32: ADJECTIVES AND ADVERBS

Underline the correct modifiers in each of the following sentences. Check your answers at the back of the book.

1. Lucinda felt (good, well) on that (beautiful, beautifully) day.

2. Alex wanted (bad, badly) to call her and tell her how (sad, sadly) he felt.

3. Sydney told her sister that she dressed (good, well) for such a (good, well) day.

4. After coming to a (sudden, suddenly) stop, Lance's (new, newly) sports car screeched (loud, loudly).

5. Stomping (forceful, forcefully) out of the room, Leigh flipped her (thick, thickly) blonde hair out of her (cool, coolly) eyes.

Misplaced Modifiers

The rule for modifiers is simple: Place the modifier as close as possible to the noun it modifies.

Why? This makes a sentence clear and precise. If you carelessly move modifiers all around your sentences, you will confuse your readers.

Look at these two sentences.

> He only voted for David for class president. (meaning he didn't help with the campaign)
> He voted only for David for class president. (meaning he didn't vote for anyone else)

What about this sentence?

> Do you ever remember seeing such a wonderful U2 concert?

or

> Do you remember ever seeing such a wonderful U2 concert?

If you're modifying the verb *seeing*, put the adverb *ever* before and as close to the verb as possible. The second sentence probably comes closer to your intended meaning.

To help you remember the importance of the place-
ment of modifiers, keep in mind the variety of meanings of this sentence.

> Only I hit Mr. McGoogle in the jaw. (Nobody
> else hit him.)
> I only hit Mr. McGoogle in the jaw. (I didn't
> also stuff him in the trash can.)
> I hit only Mr. McGoogle in the jaw. (I didn't hit
> anyone else.)
> I hit Mr. McGoogle only in the jaw. Or I hit Mr.
> McGoogle in the jaw only. (I didn't hit him any-
> where else.)

PART 3

Even More Knowledge:
Hands-on Variety

CHAPTER 6

Nine common Grammar Errors

Before we get to these common errors, let me ask a question that sounds as if I'm changing the subject. (I'm not.)

> **Question:** What's the proper way to eat fried chicken?
> **Answer:** Depends on where you are.

If you're at a picnic, you're supposed to grab the chicken with your hands. But at a formal banquet, you better start grappling with that silver dinner knife and fork! How you eat at home depends on how formal your family asks you to be at the table.

Grammar works much the same way. Standards of correctness are defined by the occasion. Even the way you speak is defined by the occasion. Think of this: If you're joking around with your friends, you speak in a different way from the way you speak with, say, the principal of your school. "Yo, wait up" works in one situation, while "I'll be there in three minutes, Mr. Shattuck" may be more appropriate for the other. Grammar and usage work the same way. We have the "picnic" variety of grammar, and we have the equivalent of the event with the two knives and the three forks. Then, there's everything in between.

Generally speaking, standards for spoken English are lower than standards for written English. When you're having a conversation, most people won't even notice small slip-ups in your speech, or if they notice them, they forgive them. In slightly more formal speaking situations and most writing situations, educated people will notice and mentally label some types of errors. In table manner terms, these are the equivalent of, say, glugging directly from the mouth of the ketchup bottle! Let's look at a couple of these.

IN SPEECH

Common Error #1: Pronoun Case

Using the wrong form of the pronoun is the first common error we'll tackle. (Reviewing the material on pages 88–92 at this point is a good idea.) This error takes on two forms:

1. Using *I, we,* or *they* when *me, us,* or *them* is correct.

2. The opposite: Using *me, us,* or *them* when *I, we,* or *they* is correct.

Examples of errors:

> This is strictly a matter for Paul and I to decide.

Wrong! It should be:

> This is strictly a matter for Paul and me to decide.

Or this one:

May Kristin and me go to the nurse's office?

Wrong! It should be:

May Kristin and I go to the nurse's office?

As you may have noticed, both of these sentences use the pronoun with another word: *Paul* and *I*, *Kristin* and *me*. That's when many errors creep in. You would never have said, "This is strictly a matter for I to decide" or "May me go to the nurse's office?" In this kind of sentence, you can let your inner ear think about what you would have said if only one person had been involved. So if you'd say, "May I go to the nurse's office?" you'd say "May Kristin and I go the nurse's office?"

The more official explanation is that personal pronouns in English are one of the few types of words that change their form depending on how they're used. (The technical word for their form is *case*.) You just have to learn which case you use in which situation.

First, the easiest part: *It* and *you* never change. So, you have to deal with only five pairs that could confuse you. Let's make it six, by adding *who* and *whom*. Review the chart below. (You saw a version of it earlier in Chapter 3.)

Nominative (Subject) Pronouns Singular
I, he, she, who

Plural
we, they, who

As the chart indicates, you use *I, he, she, we, they,* and *who* when the words are used as the **subject** of the sentence (or, in the case of *who,* its own clause): "I may go to the movies." "May I go to the movies?" "May Taylor and I go to the movies?" "He is my friend." "He and Ross are my friends." "Maggie and she are coming for dinner." "Do we have time to stop for some food?" "Could they have forgotten?" "Who is coming to dinner?" "Guess who is coming to dinner." In each of these situations, the pronoun is the subject of a verb. The chart gives you the technical term: *nominative case*). If you run all of these by your figurative inner ear, here's betting that only the compounds (Taylor and I, He and Ross, Maggie and she) made you think twice.

Now look at the chart for the form you use when the pronoun is used as any kind of object (object of a preposition or direct or indirect object). (The chart gives you the technical term: *objective case*.)

Objective (Object) Pronouns Singular
Me, her, him, whom

Plural
us, them, whom

Read each of the following:

> Maria saw *me* last night.
> The class nominated *her*.
> The class nominated *her* and *him*.
> The fans like *us*.
> Did Natalie call *them* yesterday?
> The Community Service Club gave *him* the flowers.
> Tell *me* the answer!
> Tell *her* and *me* the answer.
> You will report to *them*.

Again, your inner ear probably listened twice only to the compounds *her and him* and *her and me*.

Practice on the six sentences below. Are they correct or incorrect? If incorrect, how would you make it right?

1. Sarah and him are going to the movies.

2. Did you see Laurie and her there?

3. Give that package to Ms. Mandell and he.

4. Mr. Desiderio told Emma and I how good our papers were.

5. Lindsay met up with her friends. She and they went to get sandwiches.

6. May I ask whom is speaking?

Here's an instant answer check for the questions above:

1. Wrong! You'd say, "*He* is going to the movies," so the case doesn't change just because Sarah is involved. Correct version: *Sarah and he are going to the movies.*

2. Correct. You'd say, "Did you see her?" So *Did you see Laurie and her?* is correct.

3. Wrong! You'd say, "Give that package to him," So, *Give it to Ms. Mandell and him* is correct.

4. Wrong! You'd say, "Mr. D. told me," So, *He told Emma and me* is correct.

5. Correct. You'd say, "They went to get sandwiches," So, *She and they went* is correct.

6. Wrong! *Who* is the subject of the verb *is speaking.* A pronoun always takes its case from its own clause. (The three words *who is speaking* work together as a noun clause that is the direct object of *may ask.*)

Now you're ready for a quiz to practice what you've learned.

QUIZ #33: PRONOUN CASE

Underline the correct form of the pronoun in each of the following sentences where you have a choice. Check your answers at the back of the book.

Hercules Looks for Some Respect

Hercules, the strong man of Mt. Olympus, was in a grumpy mood. (He, Him) couldn't decide what Zeus and the other gods thought of (he, him). So he decided to ask them. He believed Artemis, the goddess of hunting, admired both her brother Apollo and (he, him, himself). What, though, did Athena, the goddess of wisdom, think? He would check things out with both Artemis and (she, her).

"Hey, Artemis," he began, tossing his cloak of lion skin around his shoulders. "Give (I, me) a straight answer. What do you think of (I, me)?"

"People always ask (I, me) questions like this," she said, annoyed. "(Who, whom) do they think they are?

But since it's you, Hercules, I'll answer. You're exactly the kind of guy I'd like to have go along on a hunt with my friends and (I, me, myself.) You're strong and capable. If I hurt (me, myself), I know you'd help. And (who, whom) has a cooler lion skin than you?"

"Thanks, Arty. Would Athena give you and (I, me) the same answer?"

"I'm not sure," said Artemis. "Why don't (we, us) curious Olympians go over to her place and ask (she, her, herself)?"

"Just between you and (I, me)," replied Hercules, "I'm a little scared of (she, her). Can you and (I, me) together be as intelligent as (she, her) is?"

"Everyone has different positive traits," Artemis replied. "Athena and (I, me) are different, but we get along. Muster up your famous courage, and may no god bother you or (I, me) on the way there. To be certain, shall (we, us) just make (we, us, ourselves) invisible?"

Common Error #2: The "Elegant Error"

Error: I felt badly for him when he lost the race.

Correction: I felt bad for him when he lost the race.

Some teachers call this the "elegant error" because it's usually made when someone tries *too* hard not to make a mistake. Somewhere along the way this speaker has probably been corrected for saying, "I did bad on the test." Yes, in *that* sentence the speaker should have said, "I did badly on the test." So, what's the difference? Here's the difference: A verb like *did* or *scored* or *performed* is an action verb and needs the adverb form of *badly*. But the verb *feel*, as used in the sentence above is a "state of being" verb, a first cousin of *am* or *is*. So, I am *bad* at playing the drums and I felt *bad* for him when he lost the race. But I play the drums *badly* and he ran *badly* in the race.

Memory tip: Avoid the "elegant error" by thinking of this silly situation. The only correct usage of the phrase *feeling badly* would be this: Put duct tape on all your fingertips and then try to determine the texture of the wall. You'll find you *feel badly*. Here, *feel* is an action verb, but you'll have many more occasions for the "state of being" use of *feel*.

Let's do a quick checkup with our friends over there on Mt. Olympus. We left Hercules and Artemis walking toward the chamber of Athena.

Underline the correct word wherever you have a choice. Check your answers at the back of the book.

"Good day, Athena," began Hercules. "I feel (bad, badly) to ask you this outright, but do you think I'm a cool guy?"

"Oh, Hercules, I'm the one who feels (bad, badly)," the goddess of wisdom wisely replied. "I've never seen you perform (bad, badly) at anything! I remember how you killed that fire-breathing bull, Cacus. I would have felt (terrible, terribly) if it had been the other way around. Did you bring Artemis with you to protect (you, yourself) from scary old (I, me)? Now that does make me feel (bad, badly)!"

IN WRITING

We move now from common errors in spoken English to errors in written English. And remember our basic principle: The more formal the situation, the more "standard" your usage of English should be. Here's an extreme example: If you're texting or e-mailing close buddies, they're happy to hear from you and aren't judging your English. But your English teacher won't be happy if you write a report that says, "*Travels with Charley* was written l8r in Steinbeck's career." Let's move on to look at seven common errors in written English.

Common Error #3: Dangling Participle

A participial phrase without a home is a dangling modifier.

> Driving down the lonely road, my mind wandered and I veered off into a ditch.

Do you know what's wrong with this sentence? It may sound just fine, but look closely at the opening phrase, *Driving down the lonely road.* Who or what was driving down the lonely road? Well, it sounds like *my mind* was driving, because that's the closest thing to the modifying phrase. But a mind can't drive itself, so something is wrong. Reword to make it clearer:

> My mind wandered as I drove down the lonely road and I veered off into a ditch.

or

> Driving down the lonely road, I let my mind wander and I veered off into a ditch.

You may discover you haven't even written the word you are describing. For example:

> While eating chocolate chip cookies, the front door blew open.

Now, who or what was eating chocolate chip cookies? *The front door*? *The front door* is the subject of the sentence. If you want to be clear that you were eating the chocolate chip cookies and not some scary cookie monster of a front door, change the sentence around:

> While I was eating chocolate chip cookies, the front door blew open.

or

> While eating chocolate chip cookies, I saw the front door blow open.

Here's another example:

> After finishing the race, my shoes stank.

Again, who or what finished the race? *My shoes*? Did your shoes run without your feet? No! So change it to:

> After I finished the race, my shoes stank.

or

> After finishing the race, I knew my shoes stank.

How could you make the following sentence clearer?

> To make a model rocket, hard work and precision is required.

Who's making that rocket? Try the following:

> To make a model rocket, you must work hard and use precision.

Now try your hand at this quiz. Remember the participial phrase acts as an adjective. Your sentence must state the word that the phrase modifies and the phrase must appear close to it.

QUIZ #35: MISPLACED MODIFIERS

Underline the misplaced modifier, and then rewrite each of the following sentences. Check your answers at the back of the book.

1. Approaching his favorite TV star, admiration was oozing out of Vincent.

_____

_____

_____

_____

2. Hearing the voice of her beloved, a wave of excitement came over Lou.

_____

_____

_____

_____

3. Riding in the back of the jeep, the moon looked beautiful.

_____

_____

_____

4. While kissing her, his wallet fell out of his back pocket.

_____

_____

_____

_____

Common Error #4:
Unparallel Parallelism

As you know from your study of math, parallel lines are straight lines that run along exactly the same distance from each other. (For example, the double *l's* in *parallel* are parallel with one another.) If one of those lines got squiggly and curvy or moved closer and then farther away from its partner, the lines wouldn't be parallel anymore.

In English, we use the term *parallel* to refer to the consistency of word forms used in certain situations. For example, if I say, "I like to skate, ski, and swim," I've correctly used a consistent or parallel form of the word for the three things I like. If I'd said, "I like skating, skiing, and to swim," I would have made an error in parallelism. Here are two more examples.

> **Wrong:** The child reacted to the red balloon eagerly and with joy.
> **Correct:** The child reacted to the red balloon eagerly and joyfully.
> **Correct:** The child reacted to the red balloon with eagerness and joy.

The child reacted in two ways; the form you choose for each needs to be parallel. You're equally correct with two adverbs or with two prepositional phrases, but not a combination of the two. (Think of an error in parallelism as being like wearing stripes with polka dots.)

> **Wrong:** Mr. Berkowitz told me that my report needed more documentation and to correct the grammatical errors.
>
> **Correct:** Mr. Berkowitz told me that my report needed more documentation and correction of the grammatical errors.
>
> **Even Smoother:** Mr. Berkowitz told me to add more documentation to my report and to correct my grammatical errors.

Practice on these five sentences below. (Hint: One is correct as is.)

1. George behaved childishly and foolishly as well as like an idiot.

2. To sail across the ocean and a book dedicated to me are my dreams.

3. If I could speak Spanish fluently and correctly, I'd be happy.

4. Here are three important rules for a good research paper: have a strong thesis, good information, and write clearly.

5. I really dislike people who interrupt me, loud gum popping, and not being a good sport.

Here's an instant answer check for the questions above:

1. Correction: George behaved childishly, foolishly, and idiotically.

2. Correction: To sail across the ocean and to have a book dedicated to me are my dreams. OR Sailing across the ocean and having a book dedicated to me are my dreams.

3. It's correct! *Fluently* and *correctly* are both adverbs that describe the action verb *could speak*. *Happy* is an adjective that goes with the linking verb in a separate part of the sentence.

4. Correction: Here are three important rules for a good research paper: have a strong thesis, gather good information, and write clearly.

5. I really dislike people who interrupt me, people who pop their gum, and people who aren't good sports.

If you had trouble with any of those, review the answers and then try the quiz below.

Correct the error in parallelism in each of the following sentences.

1. Hercules was wearing a loincloth, a lion skin, and having goatskin sandals.

   _____

   _____

2. Athena tried to put him at ease in two ways: by complimenting him and she reminded him of how he had defeated Cacus the bull.

   _____

   _____

3. After listening to the dialogue between Athena and Hercules, Artemis wondered whether to speak up and how she might begin.

   _____

   _____

4. Athena's robe pictured a scary image of the Gorgon Medusa, whose glance could turn a beast to stone or will threaten even a bold hero who stared at her too long.

_____

_____

5. Medusa's head was covered with clusters of serpents, both immature and adults.

_____

_____

Common Error #5: Faulty Comparison

There are two subcategories of errors that fall under faulty comparison. They are the comparison of two items as opposed to comparison of three or more items and a comparison that is unclear. First up is the two-versus-three-or-more category. Look at these two correct sentences:

Sentence 1: I'd have to say that Andrea is more intelligent than James.

Sentence 2: Andrea is the most intelligent student in the entire eighth grade.

The situation in sentence 1 compares Andrea with one other person, so we use the comparative form. Sometimes, as here, you use the word *more* with the adjective; if the adjective is short, the correct procedure may be to add the suffix *-er* to it. For example, we'd say "Andrea is smarter than James." In sentence 2, Andrea's intelligence is being compared to the intelligence of all the other eighth graders, so we go to the superlative form. It may involve, as it does here, the word *most* with the adjective. If the adjective is shorter, we might add the suffix *-est* to it. For example, we'd say, "Andrea is the smartest student in the entire eighth grade." The eighth grade could consist of 300 students, 30 students, or 3 students, but we'd still use the superlative form. (Nobody's quite sure why this different form for the comparison of two people or things exists, but the situation could be worse—ancient Greek had an entirely separate verb form that had to be used when two people or things were involved!)

Practice on these three sentences. Hint: One is correct as is.

1. See those two oranges on the table? Give me the biggest one.

2. Which ballerina is shortest—Kyra or Zara? And which is the more graceful?

3. I admire Joe DiMaggio more than any other player in the history of baseball.

Here is an instant answer check for the questions above:

1. Correction: See those two oranges on the table? Give me the *bigger* one. (We're comparing only *two*.)

2. Correction: Which ballerina is *shorter*—Kyra or Zara? (We're comparing only *two* of them.) The second sentence is, therefore, correct as is.

3. Correct as is. A little tricky—Joltin' Joe (one player) is being compared with all other players taken as a group, so two things are being compared. If we'd wanted to compare DiMaggio with every other player, looked at separately, the sentence might have read like this: "Of all the guys who've ever played baseball, Joe DiMaggio is the one I admire the most."

The second subcategory of comparison error are faulty because they allow for more than one interpretation. (You saw one like this earlier in this book.)

> **I'd have to say I like Chuck more than you.**

Does the speaker prefer Chuck to the person she's addressing? Or does she merely like Chuck more than the person she's addressing likes Chuck? The context may help us interpret the sentence. Still, avoid any possibility of misunderstanding by rewriting the sentence:

> **I'd have to say I like Chuck more than you do.**

> **I'd have to say I like Chuck more than I like you.**

Another variety of unclear comparison is a sentence like this:

> The weather in California is very much like Florida.

We get the general idea, but as written language, it's rather imprecise: The sentence seems to be comparing the weather in one state with another entire state! Better wording would be either "The weather in California is very much like that in Florida" or "California's weather is very much like Florida's weather" or even "California's weather is very much like Florida's." In this last version, the word *weather* in reference to Florida is clearly implied and clearly understood.

One more type: Which of these is right?

> I like chocolate brownies better than any sweet treat.
> I like chocolate brownies better than any other sweet treat.

The second one, of course. Because brownies themselves are a sweet treat, you can't compare them with themselves.

Time for some practice. (Hint: One of these sentences is correct as is.)

1. Did you like the characters in the old television show *Homicide* more than *Law & Order*?

2. Was its storyline better than *Law & Order*?

3. My parents liked Lenny Briscoe's partners less than me.

4. Do you prefer Sam Waterston's acting style in the courtroom scenes to Michael Moriarty's?

5. Angelo likes courtroom dramas better than any type of television program.

6. My brother likes television detectives even more than movies.

Here is an instant answer check for the questions above:

1. Correction: Did you like the characters in the old television show *Homicide* more than those in *Law & Order*? (You don't want to compare characters on one show with another entire show.)

2. Correction: Was its storyline better than that of *Law & Order*? Or... than *Law & Order's*?

3. Correction: My parents liked Lenny Briscoe's partners less than I did.

4. It's Correct! We know "acting style" is understood after "Michael Moriarty's."

5. Correction: Angelo like courtroom dramas better than any other type of television program.

6. Correction: My brother likes television detectives even more than movie detectives. OR My brother likes detectives on television even more than those in movies.

Review your answers to that quick checkup and then try this quiz.

QUIZ #37: FAULTY COMPARISONS

Find and correct three errors in the paragraph below. Check your answers at the back of the book.

John Steinbeck's list of prizes is a lot like William Faulkner. They both won the Nobel Prize for Literature. By the way, did you like Steinbeck's *Of Mice and Men* more than any of his books? Faulkner's style is not like Steinbeck. It's the most complicated and challenging to read.

_____

_____

_____

_____

Common Error #6:
Pronouns and Antecedents

TIP: The prefix *ante* means "before"—to avoid making pronoun-antecedent mistakes in your writing, remember that the noun goes before the pronoun in most well written sentences.

(It's good to review pages 100–107 at this point.) But first, let's make sure you know that four-syllable word *antecedent* and understand what it means in the world of grammar. *Antecedent* is a fancy technical term for the noun that is replaced by a pronoun. For example:

> When Keisha entered the room, we gave her a standing ovation because she had been so great in the performance of *Guys and Dolls*.

Here, the noun Keisha is replaced twice by pronouns: first, by *her* and then by *she*. So we could say Keisha is the antecedent of both pronouns.

One of the trickiest points in the world of antecedents and pronouns concerns words like *everyone/everything*, *anyone/anything*, or *each*. Technically, these are all singular, so that if I say "Everyone brought [pronoun] book," I need to replace the antecedent with a singular noun. It's correct to say, "Everyone brought his book," but that sounds a little sexist these days. And it's correct and inclusive to say, "Everyone brought his or her book," but it can be a little clunky, especially if the sentence goes on to something like, "*Everyone* brought his or her book and put it in his or her locker." So, more and more you'll hear people say "*Everyone* (singular) brought *their* (plural) book and put it in *their* (plural) locker." That usage may become more fully acceptable, but in the meantime there's a way around the problem. Avoid *everyone* and *each* and go for a plural form: "All the students brought their books and put them in their lockers." Then you have the satisfaction of using formally correct grammar while avoiding the sexism and the clunkiness. If it's important to know that each student had just one book, find another way to write the sentence: "Each student brought one favorite book from the summer reading list."

Let's practice with this sentence:

> Everyone should bring (his, his or her, their) gym clothes on Monday.

Sidestep all the pitfalls by changing the sentence to:

> All students should bring their gym clothes on Monday.

Now this one:

> Every scientist has (his, his or her, their) own way of conducting research.

Change to:

> All scientists have their own ways of conducting research.

Here's another:

> The judge instructed each lawyer to be sure (he, he or she, they) had reviewed the relevant research in the case.

Change to:

> The judge instructed the lawyers to be sure they had reviewed the relevant research in the case.

Try making this switch in the following three sentences.

1. A surgeon needs to be sure his training has prepared him for unexpected emergencies.

2. A kindergarten teacher must be friendly but always have control of her classroom.

3. Any elementary school student should know that he has the chance to become president of the country someday.

Here is an instant answer check for the questions above:

1. Surgeons need to be sure their training has prepared them for unexpected emergencies.

2. Kindergarten teachers must be friendly but always have control of their classrooms.

3. Elementary school students should know that they have the chance to become president of the country someday.

Another kind of error with antecedents occurs when being too imprecise:

> **Merrill likes her swimming class and is great at it.**

Merrill was great at swimming, not only at the swimming class. You could reword it to be clearer.

> **Merrill likes her swimming class and is a great swimmer.**

One more example:

> **Jim mended the porcelain picture frame which made me happy.**

What is the antecedent of *which*? Was it *the frame* that made me happy? No, it was the repair job. To be really clear, reword to

> **I was happy that Jim mended the porcelain picture frame.**

or

> **The fact that Jim mended the porcelain picture frame made me happy.**

Common Error #7: Subject-Verb Agreement

Review pages 106–107 to remind yourself of what you already know about subject-verb agreement. As you learned there, an error in agreement often sneaks in when the subject is followed by a phrase or a clause. You'd have no trouble with choosing the right verb in this sentence:

The boy (was/were) on the lawn.

It's *was*, of course. But if the sentence became "The boy who has three sisters (was/were) on the lawn," then your ear may get fooled by hearing the plural *sisters* as the subject of *were*. But of course the verb is still *was* because the subject is still *boy*.

Pretty easy so far? Well, it can get a lot harder. Look at this sentence.

Dotting the coast of Florida is thousands of palm trees.

Looks pretty good, right? Caught you! Your ear heard *Florida is*. Even if you were careful and had marked *of Florida* as a prepositional phrase, you may think the subject and verb were *coast is*—but you'd still be wrong. This sentence is arranged in what's called *inverted order*. In other words, a part of the verb comes before the subject. If we rearranged it in more ordinary order, it would correctly read:

> Thousands of palm trees are dotting the coast of Florida.

Here's another kind of troublesome sentence.

> There (is, are) a pencil and a pad of paper in the drawer.

If you said *are*, then congratulate yourself! Two grammatical traps lurk here: First of all, the word *there* is not the subject. It's a kind of "fill-in" word that leads off the sentence. The subject consists of the item or items that are in the drawer. How many are there? One and one make two! So the subject is plural. In short, you have to be sure you identify the subject and identify the verb in order to make them agree.

Practice on these four sentences below. (Note: One is correct as is.)

1. In the back of the book are a list of words that students studying Spanish may want to memorize.

2. The house with the bright blue shutters is prettier than most houses on the street.

3. Liver and onions are a dish that some people like and some people hate.

4. There is several reasons you should vote for Smithers.

Here is an instant answer check for the questions above:

1. Correction: In the back of the book is a list of words... The subject is *list*.

2. It's correct! Don't let those shutters fool you; the subject is *house*.

3. Gotcha! *Liver and onions* is one dish, so it's *Liver and onions is....*

4. Correction: There are several reasons you should vote for Smithers. The subject is *reasons*, and it's plural.

Got it? Here's your quiz.

QUIZ #38: SUBJECT-VERB AGREEMENT

Correct any errors you see in subject-verb agreement. Write the correct form of the verb above the incorrect word. Check your answers at the back of the book.

The Parthenon, located on the high acropolis of Athens, is a very beautiful building. There is several features that make it so striking. Lining each side is several graceful columns. Inside the structure, framed by all those columns, are a large statue of Athena herself. Her reputation for wisdom and her skill in battle was behind her great popularity. The very word *Parthenon*, which comes from the classical Greek for "maiden," refers to the unmarried Athena.

Common Error #8: Incorrect Idiom

Idiom is a term that's hard to define. Generally speaking, as we're using it here, it refers to a standard expression that doesn't have a logical explanation. Many idioms involve using the correct preposition. When you're queuing up to buy a ticket, do you get *in line* or *on line*? Most people say *in line*, but many natives of New York City say *on line*. Many other prepositional phrases don't offer this kind of flexibility. To be correct, you need to use the form that has become standard. Here are some examples of the more easily confused prepositions.

at, by

Use *by* only when you mean *past* or *by way of.*

> We went *by* school on our way to the concert.
> He stopped *at* the store after school (not *by the store*).

at, to

Use *to* for motion. When you go to a place, you are *at* it.

> Margot and I were *at* the mall all afternoon.
> We are going *to* the movies later.

at, with

Use *at* for a thing and *with* for a person.

> I was furious *with* my mother for not allowing me to go to the mall.
> I was angry *at* the new rule at school that doesn't allow us to leave campus.

between, among

Use *between* when you have two things and *among* for more than two things.

> *Between* you and me, this is the worst party I have been to this year.
> We shared the five cookies *among* the six of us.

beside, besides

Beside means *next to*. *Besides* means *in addition to*.

> I want to sit *beside* Jimmy tonight.
> I hope you'll talk to someone *besides* him.

from, off

Don't use *off* when you mean *from*. *Off of* is never correct.

> I bought the Janet Jackson CD *from* my favorite store.
> Get *off* the bus at Fourth Street to get to my house.

over, to

You cannot go *over* someone's house unless you have wings. Use the preposition *to*.

> We went *to* Marcel's new beach house last summer.
> Batgirl flew *over* our heads.

Idiomatic Prepositional Phrases That Will Impress Your Friends

Do you need to memorize these? Nope. Just read through them to see if there are any you usually use incorrectly. Try to work on them. You may also use this list as a reference when you write. Reading is one of the best ways to improve your grasp of correct idioms because your mind gets accustomed to seeing the phrases correctly used.

angry *about* (an idea, a thing): Mary Sarah was *angry about* the ridiculous situation in which she was involved.

angry *with* (a person): Nan was *angry with* Nina for causing it.

compare *to* (shows similarity): *Compared to* the *Mona Lisa*, this is a really good painting.

compare *with* (shows similarity and difference): You can't *compare* that *with* the *Mona Lisa*!

decide *on* (use with a noun): Let's *decide on* a movie.

decide *to* (use with a verb): Let's *decide to* eat out.

differ *with* (means "to disagree"): I *differ with* Mr. Isaacson about that Shakespearean sonnet.

differ *from* (means "unlike"): Mittens *differ from* hats because you wear mittens on your hands.

fail *in* (an attempt): I *failed in* my efforts to win first prize.

fail *to* (do something): Jeannette *failed to* submit her paper on time.

practice *for/to* (use when practice is a verb): I am *practicing for* the track meet. I have to *practice to* do well.

practice *of* (use when practice is a noun): The *practice of* cheating is not condoned by our school.

result *from/in* (when result is a verb): Weak fingernails r*esult from* not eating well. Not eating well *results in* weak fingernails.

result *of* (when result is a noun): This is the *result of* not eating well.

sympathy *for* (means "to feel for"): Brian had *sympathy for* Matt.

sympathy *with* (means "agreement, sharing of feelings"): Matt had *sympathy with* Brian's position in the matter.

Don't Use Prepositions with These, Please . . .

continue: I will continue my project.

Wrong: I will continue *with* my project.

inside: Paul is inside the pet house.

Wrong: Paul is inside *of* the pet house.

meet: I want to meet the exchange student.

Wrong: I want to meet *with* the exchange student (unless you mean you want to schedule a conference time).

name: Claudine was named best brain.

Wrong: Claudine was named *as* best brain.

off: I fell off the homecoming float.

Wrong: I fell off *of* the homecoming float.

visit: I am going to visit Amy this spring.

Wrong: I am going to visit *with* Amy this spring. (In some regions of the country, *visit with* is used as an acceptable synonym for *had a good talk with*: "I visited with Mrs. Mason for half an hour and really enjoyed our time together.")

If you are unsure, try to eliminate the extra preposition. If the sentence makes sense without it, you probably don't need it.

What about ending a sentence with a preposition? You may have already heard this rule. You should try to make sure your formal sentences don't end with a preposition—prepositions always take an object noun or pronoun, so if you don't have one after the open preposition, it is sort of left dangling there. You can correct this by rewording your sentence

I didn't know which house Marla lived *in*.

to

I didn't know *in* which house Marla lived.

And sometimes what fault-finders call "ending the sentence with a preposition" isn't that at all. For example, "Did you go to the dictionary and look that word up?" *Up* isn't a preposition at all, just part of the two-word verb *look up* which means *to consult a reference*. So, don't worry too much about this old rule about not ending a sentence with a preposition. It's one of those old-timey rules that isn't a big deal these days except in the most formal of writing. In terms of our comparisons with table manners, if it isn't quite a fingerbowl, it's a pickle fork.

Underline the correct preposition in each of the following sentences. Check your answers at the back of the book.

1. The Greek hero Theseus went (to, by) the island of Crete to save people from a monster called the minotaur, who lived in the center of a maze.

2. The minotaur differed (from, with) many foes: He was half human, half bull.

3. Theseus was able to slay the minotaur and then find his way out of the maze with a thread he got (off of, from) Ariadne, the daughter of the king of Crete.

4. He must have been (inside, inside of) the maze for over an hour.

5. (Beside, Besides) killing the minotaur, Theseus performed other valiant feats.

6. Shakespeare's use of Theseus as a character in his play *A Midsummer Night's Dream* was the result (of, from) centuries of retelling of stories about him.

Common Error #9: Incorrect Diction

Diction is just a fancy way of referring to the choice of words to fit a certain context. Using the right word at the right time not only shows how brilliantly you speak and write, but also makes your speaking and writing clearer and more precise. If you use the wrong word, people will think your speech or writing is sloppy, or they may misunderstand your meaning. The following words are among those most commonly misused. You may hear many of them used incorrectly every week.

absolutely

Do you mean *yes*? If you're writing, better to use the simpler, more direct word.

affect/effect

Affect is a verb. It means "to influence." You can *affect* a situation in which you are involved. Your teacher can *affect* your grade in English. Your mother can *affect* your ideas about life.

Effect is usually a noun, meaning "result." The *effect* was stunning. The special *effect* in the movie was spectacular.

Effect can sometimes be used as a verb as well—if it is, it means "to accomplish." The new principal hoped to *effect* a number of changes in the school.

Note: In the last few years, people have begun to use *impact* as a verb (perhaps to avoid choosing between *affect* and *effect*). It's gaining acceptance, but careful users still frown on those who say, "How will this *impact* our class trip?" or, even worse, something grotesque like, "The computer has been very *impactful* in the last 20 years."

aggravate/irritate

You *aggravate* a situation. You *irritate* a person. *Aggravate* means to "make something worse." If your mother tells you that you're *aggravating* her, you can tell her that, no, in fact, you are *irritating* her. Won't that do the trick? Tommy was *irritated* by his aunt's frequent nagging about his hair. The skin rash was *aggravated* by the lotion.

agree to/agree with

You *agree to* something and *agree with* someone. Helen *agreed with* John. They *agreed to* stop fighting for just one day.

ain't

Ain't no such word. Always use *isn't* instead: There *isn't* any reason for you to do poorly on the test.

allusion/illusion

When you refer to something indirectly, that's an *allusion*. An *illusion* is that rabbit out of a hat trick. Her speech was sprinkled with *allusions* to all the famous people she had met. Making the Statue of Liberty disappear was one of David Copperfield's greatest *illusions*.

alot/a lot

You say *a little*, right? Why should *a lot* be made into one word? There is no such word as *alot*. She had *a lot* of reasons not to do her homework. Or just avoid it and say *many*.

all together/altogether

All together means "together as a group." *Altogether* means "completely." We were *all together* this year for Thanksgiving. You are *altogether* right about that one!

among/between

Use *among* when you are talking about more than two things. Use *between* only when referring to two things. If you have two groups, you may also use *between,* even though there may be a lot of people in each group. The slimy fight *between* the citizens of Butterville and Margarinetown continued for many years. *Between* you and me, that was the worst fish I've ever eaten. There was a dispute *among* the students in the history class.

Affect vs. Effect
Here's an easy way to remember the difference between *affect* and *effect*. *Affect* is a verb. We know that verbs are action words. *Affect* and *action* both begin with *a*. So, action can help you remember that *affect shows action*.

Effect is a noun or a thing. An *effect* is the result or consequence of an action. Think of the phrase *cause and effect* to remember that an effect is an outcome.

as/like

Use *as* when you are comparing phrases and *like* when you are comparing nouns and pronouns. She's almost as smart *as* I am. He's just *like* his brother. *As* in the sixth volume of the Harry Potter series, the plot of the seventh volume darkens as it goes along.

at this point in time

Just say *at this time.* (Does time really have "points"?)

basically

Avoid this word whenever you can. It's not technically wrong, but it is overused. Often, you don't need it at all. Instead of "*Basically,* I'm in it for the money," you could just say, "I'm in it for the money."

being that/being as

These sound pretentious. Remember that the point is to be clear and precise. Just say *because*. *Because* I want to do well, I am avoiding silly-sounding phrases.

beside/besides

Beside means *next to*. *Besides* means *in addition to*. Try not to mix them up. "I was hoping to sit *beside* Jake," Callie said. You have a lot to worry about *besides* Karla.

between you and . . . ?

Okay, once and for all: The correct phrase is *between you and me*, not *between you and I*. Remember that *between* is a preposition, so it always takes an object pronoun. *Between you and me*, this is the most delicious slop I've ever eaten.

bring/take

You *bring* things to the person who is speaking. You *take* things away from the person who is speaking. *Bring* me the head of Caesar! "*Take* this tray to your mother," said Dad. "*Bring* me the tray!" yelled Mom.

borrow/lend

Same idea as above: You *borrow* from someone; you *lend* to someone. May I *borrow* your book? I'll *lend* it to you.

can/may

People often use *can* when they mean *may*. Asking if you *can* leave the room is asking if you have the ability to leave the room. Use *can* if you want to know if you are able to do something. Use *may* if you want to ask for permission. "*Can* I eat 280 cherry pies?" wondered Beatrice. "*May* I watch her try?" asked Beatrice's sister, Lilly.

can't hardly

Hardly is a negative word. If you *can't hardly*, then you can. What you want to say is *can hardly*. The same is true for *can barely*. I *can barely* keep my eyes open. I *can hardly* wait for my birthday.

compare/contrast

You *compare* things when you think about their similarities and differences. If you are *contrasting* things, you are only looking at how they are different from each other. The teacher asked us to *compare* the characters in the books we are reading. The *contrast* between Ms. Hoffmeyer and Mr. Zinger is striking—she is so laid-back and he is so tense!

compare with/compare to

Compare with is generally used when you have two equal things and you want to point out differences. *Compare to* is used to point out similarities. *Compared with* Mr. Wylie's class, Ms. Smith's is a breeze! Shall I *compare* thee to a summer's day?

complement/compliment

To *complement* with an *e* means to go together with. To *compliment* with an *i* means to say nice things about. You can remember the difference by thinking that I like to receive *compliments*. Spaghetti *complements* meatballs so perfectly. Mr. Smyth *complimented* my use of perfect grammar.

could of

It's always wrong. The right thing to say is *could have.* The same holds true for *would of* or *should of.* I *could have* been a contender!

further/farther

Farther refers to time and quantity measurements. Use *further* to mean *more.* He couldn't go any *farther* on the trail after he sprained his ankle. Laurice wanted to have *further* discussion about the new rules.

fewer/less

Fewer refers to things that can be counted. *Less* refers to a general quantity. This one's fun, because you can catch many teachers asking for "five pages or *less,*" when they should be asking for "five pages or *fewer.*" How about those express lines at the supermarket? How many signs can you spot that say "ten items or *less*"? (That's wrong!) I'd like *fewer* french fries and *less* mashed potatoes. Give me *fewer* egg rolls and *less* soup. *More* money and *fewer* pennies.

former/latter

Former refers to the first of two things, and *latter* refers to the second or last of the two. You can remember these because *former* begins with an *f* just like *first* and *latter* begins with an *l* just like *last*. Money and health: the *former* can make you comfortable, but only the *latter* can make you feel good.

goes

Do you mean *says*? If you say things like, "So, she *goes*, 'Get outta here!'" then stop it! Don't say *goes* unless you are talking about someone going somewhere. If you are telling someone what someone else said, use the right word, *says*. Mary Ann *says*, "Get out of my face!"

healthful/healthy

If you lead a *healthful* life, you will be *healthy*. *Healthful* refers to something that gives you health or leads to good health. People, plants, and animals can be *healthy*. Diet, climates, and exercise programs can be *healthful*. I stopped eating potato chips, and now I feel so *healthy*. But my new *healthful* life is just no fun.

hopefully

In the strictest usage, *hopefully* means *with hope*. For example, you wait *hopefully* for the results of your test (meaning that you are waiting with hope). Technically, you shouldn't say "*Hopefully*, we will come here tomorrow," when you mean "*I hope* we will come here tomorrow." The new use of *hopefully* is becoming more acceptable, but really careful language users still avoid it. So, own your own hope: *I hope* to do well on my exam. *I hope* the Yankees have a good season. If you're desperate for just one word, try *ideally* or use the phrase *with a little luck. With a little luck,* it won't rain on our parade.

imply/infer

If you *imply* something, you are hinting at it. You *infer* something when you figure it out. If your father *implies* that you need a haircut, you might *infer* that he doesn't like your style. Mr. Katzenjammer *implied* that we would have a pop quiz tomorrow. Tammy *inferred* from Joe's nervous behavior that he liked her.

immigrate/emigrate

To *immigrate* is to move to a new country. You *emigrate* from the country you are leaving. Think of the *immigrants*—they were coming to the United States. The *immigrants* of the early 1900's came to Ellis Island. They *emigrated* from Ireland during the great Potato Famine.

in regards to

Use *regarding* or *in regard to* (no *-s*). *Regarding* your letter, I will be there on the 14th.

intelligent/intelligible

Intelligent means smart. If something is *intelligible*, it is understandable. Lionel's speech was *intelligent;* he made references to all the books in our course. Rose's speech was *intelligible;* she spoke clearly and loudly.

irregardless

No such word. Say *regardless*. *Regardless* of what you think, I am going to dye my hair green.

Than vs. Then

The words *then* and *than* are often confused, both in writing and in speech. This rhyme can help you decide which word you need to use:

Choose the word **then,** if you're discussing **when.**

Then means "at that time." Notice that *then* and *when* have similar spellings. This can help you remember that *then* tells *when.*

Than is a conjunction that is used to compare two or more things. Remember that *than* is spelled with an *a.*

it's/its

It's is a contraction meaning *"it is."* We know it's confusing, but *its* is the possessive form of the pronoun *it*. Remember that none of the possessive pronouns take *-'s*. Think of *his, hers, theirs, ours*—none of them uses an *-'s*. *It's* so difficult to keep all these chairs straight. That chair is broken; *its* leg is cracked in the middle.

lay/lie

These are confusing. Check out the section on weird verbs (page 117–120). *Lay* means to set down. *Lie* means to recline. *Lay* the book on the table. *Lie* on the couch.

like

I *like* you. I felt *like* an idiot. These uses of *like* are fine. Just try not to use *like* as a "filler" word over and over in your speech. *Like*, when is the test?" or "When is she, *like*, going to class?" Like eating junk food (that *like* is okay), using an occasional slangy *like* is fine, but if you get used to saying it all the time, it will come out even when you don't want it to. Practice with friends in a 10-minute conversation. Every time an inappropriate *like* slips out, the offending person forfeits a quarter (or a nickel or a penny).

many/much

Same as *fewer/less*. Use *many* for things that can be counted and *much* for a general quantity. *Many* of the people at the party were pigs. *Much* of the dip was gone by the time I got to the buffet table.

most

Be careful not to use this word when you mean *almost*. Don't say, "*Most* everyone was there." *Almost* everyone was there.

nauseated/nauseous

Many people say *nauseous* when they mean *nauseated,* and the world is beginning to accept the change. But you'll definitely be right if you observe the following distinction. If you are *nauseous,* you make someone sick. If you are *nauseated,* you feel sick. If something is *nauseous,* it makes you *nauseated.* The smell of rotten eggs is *nauseous.* She was *nauseated* by the idea of eating the pet fish.

number/amount

Same as *fewer/less*. *Number* refers to things that can be counted. *Amount* refers to a quantity of things that cannot be counted separately. I have a *number* of dollars in my wallet. The *amount* of money she spends is mind-blowing! The *number* of eggs in the recipe was reduced. The *amount* of milk was increased.

persecuted/prosecuted

If you *persecute* someone, you annoy them excessively. To *prosecute* means "to be brought before a court of law." I think Mr. Van Dam is trying to *persecute* me with all this homework! This country believes that criminals should be *prosecuted* for their crimes.

principle/principal

The *principal* of your school is your pal—it ends in *pal. Principal* also functions as an adjective meaning "most important." A *principle* is a rule or a guideline. The *principal* reason *Principal* Green was there was to help out. His *principles* inspire him to help people.

respectively/respectfully

Respectively means "in that order." *Respectfully* means "with respect." Some people sign letters *respectfully yours*. The most important things in life are health, happiness, and money, *respectively*. I submit this application to you *respectfully*.

snuck

No way! You'll hear it, but the formally correct past tense form of *sneak* is *sneaked*: She *sneaked* down the hall, past her sleeping parents, and off to the party.

stationary/stationery

Remember that *stationery* with an *e* goes into an envelope (which starts with *e*) and is sold in a *stationery* store. *Stationary* with an *a* means staying still: The spider remained *stationary* for hours, waiting for its prey. Our local *stationery* store sells the prettiest blue *stationery*.

too/to

Too is an adverb meaning *also* or *more than enough*. *To* is a preposition—use it to place a noun. We are going *to* my house after dinner. You are *too* much!

ultimate

Use *ultimate* to mean *final.* Don't use *ultimate* to mean "the best," as in the "*ultimate* taste sensation!" You'll sound like a commercial. They finally reached their *ultimate* destination—home.

you're/your

People get this one wrong all the time. *You're* is a contraction meaning *you are. Your* is the possessive form of the pronoun *you. You're* invited to the party! *Your* puppy is so cute.

Underline the correct word or words in each of the following sentences. Check your ansers at the back of the book.

1. Odysseus's trick on the Cyclops made that one-eyed giant so angry he was barely (intelligent, intelligible).

2. "(Your, You're) name is Noman?" said the Cyclops. "(Its, It's) the first time I've heard that name."

3. The Cyclops's brutal practice of eating men he disliked was more than (aggravating, irritating) to Odysseus.

4. The Greek hero remained in a (stationary, stationery) position in the Cyclops's cave to lessen the chances of being grabbed and consumed for dinner.

5. If Odysseus had lost (fewer, less) men to the Cyclops, he would have been happier.

6. "While I'd like to (lie, lay) down and nap," said Odysseus to himself, "I've got to think up a way to get out of this cave."

7. "Yes, (its, it's) true," said Odysseus later. "I (snuck, sneaked) out of the cave by holding on tightly to fleece on the underbelly of a giant ram. "

The School of Redundancy School

A redundancy error occurs when you repeat yourself or use words that are not necessary. The following phrases are redundant. Try to avoid using them.

> **4 A.M. in the morning**—A.M. means "in the morning." P.M. means "at night." Don't say 9 P.M. at night either.

At this point in time—Just say "at this time," or how about plain old "now"?

An approximate guess—You either approximate or you guess. Same thing.

Believe you me—When you say, "Believe me," the you is implied, so you don't need to include it.

Both alike—If you say simply "They are alike," you don't need to say "both."

Center around—Use center on. It makes more sense. The discussion centered on the need to hire a new teacher of Mandarin.

Circle around—If you are circling, you are going around. Just use "circle."

Consensus of opinion—Just say consensus. If you have a consensus, you have a whole bunch of opinions working together. The consensus was that Mr. Geekly was the worst teacher in the school.

Dead corpse—A corpse is dead. But you knew that, didn't you?

Estimated at about—Say either about or estimated at. The student body is estimated at 300. There are about 300 students in our school.

Game plan/plan—If you're not talking about a literal game, the phrase game plan adds nothing to "plan" except the sense of a tired cliché. Mom has worked out a plan for preparing the big Thanksgiving dinner.

He is a man who/She is a woman who—Too many words. All you need to say is "He is . . . " or "She is . . . "

Pair of twins—Avoid this, unless you are referring to two different sets of twins.

The reason is because—Say, "the reason is..." or "because..." The reason I want to finish this book is that I need to write a book report. I want to finish this book because I have to write a book report.

Too premature, too perfect, really pregnant, very unique—These things either are or aren't. You can't have varying degrees of them. You are either premature or you're not. You are either perfect or you're not. Well, you get the idea.

The year of 2008—Just say 2008.

Track record/record—Track record is a very worn-out sports metaphor for, well, record. Give that tired phrase a rest and just say, "The politician's record on health care is clear."

Cool Word History:

Capitol vs. Capital

These terms are similar in spelling and in meaning, although there are significant differences. The term for a town or city that serves as a seat of government is spelled "capital." The term for the building in which a legislative assembly meets is spelled "capitol." These words have different etymologies that might help you keep the two straight: Capital originally comes from Latin *capitlis*, from *caput*, head (or in the financial sense, as money laid out.) Capitol, the building, has its beginnings in an ancient building: Jupiter's temple in Rome. Capitoline was the hill on which Jupiter's temple stood.

True fact—A fact is true. All you need to say is fact.

As you advance in your studies, you'll become sensitive to other examples of errors in diction. Some of them can be interesting. For example, you might overhear one girl telling a classmate who recited all the presidents of the United States and their dates that he must have a *photogenic* mind. You smile quietly because you know *photogenic* means "tending to be attractive in photographs." The girl made an error in diction: She meant to say that her fellow student must have a *photographic* mind, one that learns facts easily, as if mentally photographing them.

CHAPTER 7
Diagramming Sentences

Diagramming sentences? What is it? Why would anyone want to do it?

Let's take those two questions one at a time. First, the "what." A **diagram of a sentence** is a picture of the way the parts of the sentences connect with each other. The picture is simpler than a longer explanation that uses words.

Here's a comparison: Someone in your family might have shown you a drawing called a family tree. It shows your name and the names of any brothers and sisters you might have. Above that, you have the names of your two parents and possibly their brothers and sisters, and then above that, the names of your four grandparents, and possibly the names of your eight great-grandparents. It's a picture of how you're all related.

That second question—why would anyone want to do it? Just as a diagram of a family tree saves you the trouble of saying "And the mother of my maternal grandmother was Lily Louise Oldham before she married Wayne Bombailey, Jr., and the father of my paternal grandfather was Albert Willard Wilhelm, who married…" a diagram of a sentence gives you a quick picture. This diagram shows at a glance that you are able to tell the subject, the verb, and all the other elements of a sentence.

Some people find that diagramming is challenging fun—you use your brain and you use your hands. Others argue that getting better at the step-by-step analysis required for diagramming a sentence makes them better at many different kinds of problem-solving tasks. But all students of language agree that diagramming definitely strengthens their sense of how sentences are structured. So, ready? Let's start.

TIP: When diagramming sentences remember that if you take it step by step, it's not so hard. Start with the basics—subject and verb—and build your sentence diagram from there.

We'll start with the simplest kinds of sentences. (You'll get to use knowledge you've already acquired.) Then we'll move to those that are medium, hard, and finally, the really hard sentences.

EASY SENTENCES

Step 1: Subjects and verbs. Divide the sentence into its subject and its predicate (and remember that the verb is the heart of the predicate). Everything in the complete subject is going to go to the left of a vertical dividing line. Everything in the complete predicate is going to go the right of that vertical dividing line. Let's illustrate that with a two-word sentence.

Dogs bark.

We have a noun as the subject and a verb as the predicate.

Step 2. Adjectives and adverbs. Not many sentences are going to be that simple, but we're on our way! Let's make the sentence just a little more complicated:

Hungry dogs bark loudly.

We know that *hungry* is an adjective modifying *dogs* (What kind of dogs are they? *Hungry dogs!*) So now we put the adjective modifying the subject on an oblique line under "dogs." The verb *bark* has an adverb modifying it (How do they bark? They bark *loudly*.) So we put the adverb *loudly* on a slanted line under "bark." Anyone glancing at our diagram can tell we know the subject, the verb, an adjective modifying the subject, and an adverb modifying the verb.

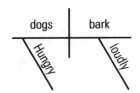

Step 3. What if the sentence is even more complicated? No problem. Just keep in mind the basic rule that the subject and everything that modifies it go to the left of the vertical line, and the verb and everything modifying it go to the right of the vertical line.

Hungry dogs in the animal shelter bark loudly at night.

We can tell that in this sentence **in the animal shelter** is telling us more about "which dogs" are the hungry dogs. We can recognize it as a prepositional phrase with a preposition, *in*, an object, *shelter* and two adjectives *the* and *animal* modifying the object. And when do those hungry dogs in the animal shelter bark loudly? They bark *at night*. So now we recognize a prepositional phrase with its preposition and its object that describes the verb. We place it, as you see below, under the verb.

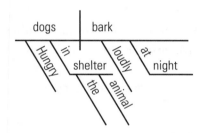

We could add as many adjectives, adverbs, and prepositional phrases as we wanted and this basic structure would still work fine. Just for fun, we'll make up a longer sentence of this kind.

> Hungry dogs with purple spots in the new animal shelter bark loudly at fast cars in the night.

Nothing changes. We just add "with purple spots" to our description of the dogs, and we add "at fast cars" to our description of how the barking occurs.

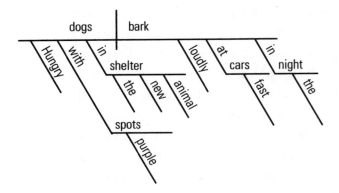

One more note: Any time you have two subjects or two verbs or both (compound subject and/or compound verb), you indicate that fact as shown below.

Cats and dogs romped in the yard.

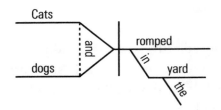

Lassie barked and begged for more doggie treats.

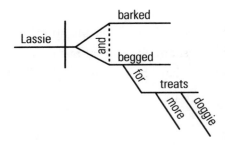

MEDIUM-HARD SENTENCES

Ready for the next challenge? What if the sentence you want to diagram has a complement? Remember, that could be a direct object, an indirect object, a predicate noun—sometimes called *predicate nominative*—or a predicate adjective. Let's leave the indirect object for last. We've got two categories of complements for our diagramming: the direct object (sometimes referred to as an *object complement*) or the predicate noun or predicate adjective (both of these are sometimes called *subject complements*).

Type 1. Let's start with a sentence with a direct object. You remember from Chapter 3 that a direct object answers the question "what?" or "whom?" about a subject and an action verb.

> Jeremy hit the ball.

In this sentence, *ball* is the direct object. To diagram a direct object, put your subject and verb in the usual spots, then, after the verb, draw a vertical line just down to your horizontal line and place the direct object after it.

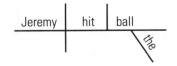

Even if we added modifiers (adjectives, adverbs, or prepositional phrases) to the subject, the verb, or the direct object, you'd know what to do.

Jeremy proudly hit the ball over the fence.

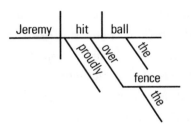

Type 2. What if we had a predicate noun or a predicate adjective? As you remember, a predicate noun comes after a linking verb and is another name for the subject: *Suzie is my friend.* The predicate adjective comes after a linking verb and describes the subject: *Suzie is friendly.* These two complements are diagrammed exactly the same way.

Place your subject and your verb in the customary way, and then draw a slanting line, one that points back toward the subject. The predicate noun or the predicate adjective goes right after that slanting line.

Suzie is my friend. or **Suzie is friendly.**

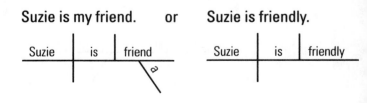

You could add adjectives or adverbs or prepositional phrases and nothing would change:

Sweet Suzie is always a good friend.

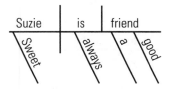

Type 3. Time to go back and pick up that indirect object. Remember two things: You'll never have an indirect object unless you also have a direct object. An indirect object, which tells you "to whom" or "for whom" something is done, functions just like a prepositional phrase—but there's no preposition. So you diagram it just the way you would diagram a prepositional phrase, but the line where the preposition would have gone is left blank. Here's a basic example.

The boy told the teacher a lie.

We've got our subject, our verb, our direct object (*lie*) and now we have an indirect object. To whom did he tell the lie? He told it to the teacher, but the preposition is omitted.

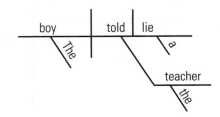

Even if we added more modifiers, nothing gets more complicated.

The guilty boy quickly told a big lie to his kindergarten teacher.

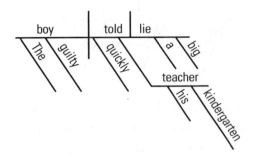

SUPER-HARD SENTENCES

Now we move to the equivalent of the super-high diving board. The most complicated kinds of sentences fall into two categories:

- Those sentences with those grammatical amphibians we call verbal phrases. (You may want to review pages 120–125 at this point.) Remember the three subdivisions: gerunds, participles, and infinitives.

- Those complex sentences with dependent clauses. (You may want to review the introductory material about complex sentences on pages 62–63.) Again, there are three subdivisions: noun clauses, adjective clauses, and adverb clauses.

Let's look at both of these one step at a time.

Category 1: Verbal phrases.

In the first category, you could have a sentence such as:

I like eating hot dogs.

I like what? *Eating hot dogs.* The direct object of *I like* is the verbal phrase *eating hot dogs. Eating,* as used here, is enough of a noun to be part of the answer to the question of "What do I like?" but it's enough of a verb to take its own direct object. So, our diagram looks a little more complicated, as we add a little "stilt" contraption to it.

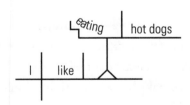

Let's try another sentence.

Sitting outside is pleasant in the summer.

What's pleasant? Not *sitting.* Not *outside.* But the verbal phrase *sitting outside. Sitting* is enough of a noun to be a part of the subject, but it's enough of a verb that it's modified by an adverb answering the question "where?" So we need our stilt contraption again, this time in the subject position.

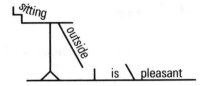

The stilt setup may also be used with a second type of verbal, the infinitive, the verbal consisting of a verb form preceded by *to*. So, if we changed the previous sentence to "I like to eat hot dogs," we'd use the same structure.

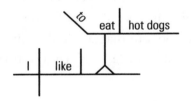

In the two sentences above, our verbal phrase was used as a noun (the technical name is *gerund*)—once as a direct object, once as a subject. Sometimes, you may remember, verbal phrases can be modifiers called participles.

Seeing the giant lizard, Zach sped down the street.

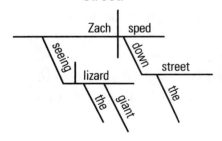

As you can see, the participle is identified in the diagram by being written on the curved angle of the line.

Or this sentence:

> Located on the bank of the Hudson River, the historic inn draws many visitors.

Which historic inn are we talking about? *The historic inn located on the banks of the Hudson River. Located* and the two phrases modifying it tell us which inn. But since *located* is a form of a verb here being used as an adjective, we indicate that fact in our diagram as shown below.

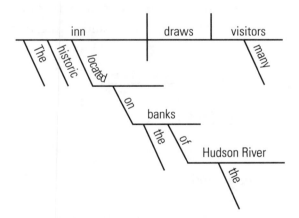

Category 2. The really complicated sentences. These are the complex sentences. Each of them has a main clause with its subject and verb, and each also has a dependent (or subordinate) clause with its own subject and verb.

You'll remember that here are three "subspecies" of these complex sentences: those with (1) noun clauses, (2) adjective clauses, and (3) adverb clauses.

Let's look at the noun clauses first because diagrams of them use the stilt contraption we know from some of the sentences with verbal phrases.

Here is a sentence with a noun clause:

I know you are my friend.

What do I know? *I know you are my friend.* The entire clause *you are my friend* serves as the direct object of *know.* It has to go into our stilt structure to show that it has its own subject, verb, and predicate noun.

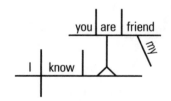

Here's another one:

That you are my friend is clear.

Something is clear. Is it the sky? No, it's *that you are my friend.* Again, we need our stilt structure to show that entire clause is the subject of the verb *is* and the predicate adjective *clear.*

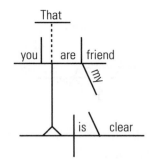

Okay, on to adjective clauses and adverb clauses. Sentences with these clauses have one thing in common: Both are diagrammed with a "two-story structure." This means there is one level for the main clause and a lower level for the adjective or adverb clause. The "stairway" between the two levels, the dotted line, attaches the dependent clause to the word it modifies in the main clause.

Let's look first at adjective clauses. These dependent clauses function just as one-word adjectives do: They answer a question (such as "which one?" or "what kind?") about a word in the main clause.

> The woman who has the long braids is my camp counselor.

Which woman is my camp counselor? The one *who has the long braids*. So, *who has the long braids* is an adjective clause describing the word *woman*.

First we diagram the main clause—all the words except the adjective clause.

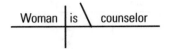

That's the main level. Now, below it, we diagram the adjective clause.

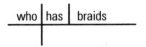

Since we know that entire second level clause modifies *woman*, we join our two levels of diagramming with a dotted line between the noun *woman* and the pronoun *who* that replaces it.

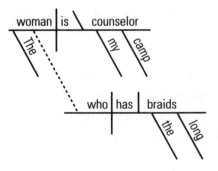

Here's another complex sentence with an adjective clause.

Andy wants a cell phone that has lots of features.

This time, the dependent clause modifies a direct object. Our main clause is *Andy wants a cell phone.* What kind of cell phone? The kind *that has lots of features.* Thus, our two-level diagram looks like this.

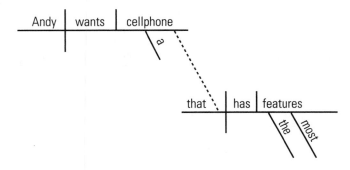

The dotted line shows us that the entire adjective clause modifies *cell phone* and it's hooked on to the pronoun that replaces *cell phone.*

Our last category of complicated sentences is the complex sentence with an adverb clause. The adverb clause answers the same questions one-word adverbs answer: "When?" or "under what circumstances?" are typical.

Here is an example:

> When Milton heard the alarm, he jumped out of bed.

Our biplane diagram will have the main clause on top (whether it comes first in the sentence or not) and the dependent adverb clause beneath it. Just as with the adjective clause, the two are joined by a dotted line. Here, though, the word that shows the relationship is written on the dotted line.

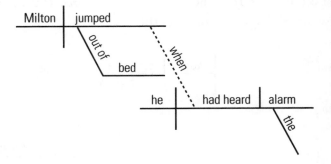

Now take a look at this one:

Milton chose another five minutes of sleep, although he had heard the buzz of the clock.

Under what circumstances did he choose those extra five minutes of sleep? Under the circumstances of having *heard the buzz of the alarm clock*. So, we write the word *although* on the dotted line joining the adverb clause to the main clause.

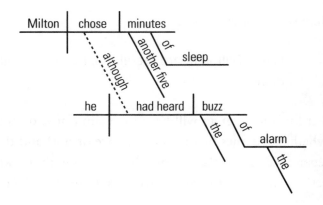

Take a deep breath! You've now covered most of the features of diagramming. You have the knowledge needed to diagram most sentences, no matter how long and complex. A sentence could have a dependent clause *and* a verbal phrase, but you'd take it step-by-step and have no problem diagramming it. As we wave a farewell to this chapter on diagramming sentences, we will examine a sentence like that. In fact, we'll diagram that very sentence.

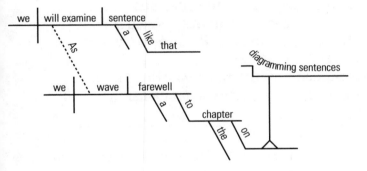

Just for fun, look at the really complicated opening sentences of the Declaration of Independence and the Preamble to the Constitution. If you wanted to diagram those sentences, you would follow the same procedures you've learned in this chapter.

Diagramming Sentences Step-By-Step

Step 1: Locate the main clause.
  —Analyze its elements: subject, verb, adjectives, adverbs, prepositional phrases, and complements. Check to see if there are any verbal phrases.
  —Diagram it.
Step 2: Identify any dependent clauses.
  —Analyze their elements, as you did with the main clause. Be sure to check for verbal phrases.
—Diagram each of them, connecting them as appropriate to the main clause.

No sweat, right? Just remember, your diagramming motto is "Step-by-step."

Read the two easy sentences, two medium sentences, and two hard sentences below. Following the "Diagramming Sentences Step-by-Step" chart above, diagram each of the sentences below. Check your answers at the back of the book.

The Easy Duo

1. The Greek gods lived on Mt. Olympus.

2. Beautiful Mt. Olympus towers over the landscape.

The Medium Duo

3. Athena gave the olive tree to the people of Greece.

4. The beautiful Aphrodite was the goddess of love.

The Hard Duo

5. Zeus sometimes liked to frighten people with his thunderbolt.

6. The owl, which was associated with Athena, appeared very wise.

CHAPTER 8
Spelling and Punctuation

LEARNING TO SPELL CORRECTLY

It's often said that some people are naturally good spellers. To a degree, that can be true. Some people do have a knack for spotting misspelled words. That's the trick; it's often a matter of learning to recognize a misspelled word, not necessarily knowing how to spell every word.

Does that seem strange? Good spellers don't automatically know how to spell everything, but they do recognize words that are misspelled. To them, misspellings just look funny. How do you cultivate this careful eye? There are two steps.

> **Step 1: Reading is probably the best way to train yourself to recognize misspelled words. Why?** The more you look at words that are spelled correctly (and let's assume that in most books the words are spelled correctly), the more you recognize incorrectly spelled words. It's like eating in good restaurants all the time—after a while, you start to know the difference between good food and bad food.

> **Step 2: Edit your own work.** Before you hand in your work, get in the habit of rereading it. Circle or mark any words that look even slightly wrong to you. How many can you spot? If you

are using a computer, try to check for misspellings manually before you use the spell-checker. You'll probably find a few misspellings. It would be really great if you looked up all those words in a dictionary, but right now, the first step is simply to train yourself to recognize words that look wrong.

Now What?

Soon, you'll notice which words you frequently misspell. Think of these misspellings as just a bad habit. Do you have some rule in your head like "*i* before *e* except after *c*," and as a result, you always spell *weird* incorrectly as *wierd*? That's understandable. You should look at the words you misspell and think up a mnemonic to remember how to spell them.

What's a Mnemonic?

A **mnemonic** (ni-MAHN-ik) is a little memory device. (The word is derived from *Mnemosyne* [ni-MAHZ-uh-nee], the Greek goddess of memory.) One example of a spelling mnemonic is "*i* before *e* except after *c*," or when it sounds like *a*, as in *neighbor* or *weigh*. You may remember the spelling of *cemetery* with the punning sentence "We get there with ease [*e*'s]." But there are other ways to remember the correct spellings of words.

Look at the part of the word you always misspell. For example, sep*e*rate is a common misspelling of sep*a*rate.

Here are some popular mnemonics you may already be using to help you remember facts about history, words, and science.

Divorced, Beheaded, Died, Divorced, Be-headed, Survived. (Mnemonic for the six wives of Henry VIII and their fates.)

Rhythm has your two hands moving! (A mnemonic for how to spell rhythm.)

Richard of York Gave Battle In Vain (A mnemonic for remembering the colors of the rainbow—Red, Orange, Yellow, Green, Blue, Indigo, Violet—in order.)

Check out the spot in the word that gives you trouble–almost everybody puts an *e* instead of an *a* in the middle. In order to remember the correct spelling, you could say to yourself: "There's *a rat* in *separate.*"

And what about *weird?* You may just remember that *weird* is, well, a weird word, so it doesn't follow the rules. It may also help to memorize this sentence: "Neither the weird financier nor the foreigner seizes leisure at its height." That one sentence has seven words that are common exceptions to the "*i* before *e* except after *c*" rule.

What If I Can't Think of a Mnemonic?

If you've tried hard but really can't think up a mnemonic for a word, we're willing to bet you memorized the spelling of the word just by thinking about it so hard. It often helps to sound out a word phonetically (pronounce the word in your head exactly the way it is spelled) if it has a strange spelling. For example, you might say the phrase *to get her* to yourself whenever you spell *together.* Or that *Connecticut* contains the sentences "Connect? I cut."

Sometimes plain old logic works. For example, the very word *misspell.* It has those two *s*'s because it's made up of the prefix *mis-* (as in *mistake*) and the word *spell.*

Don't Use Silly Spellings When You Write!

We have to put a plea in for this—don't write using fun, silly spellings, such as *nite* (instead of *night*), *thru* (instead of *through*) or *luv* (instead of *love*). These may be okay for notes or text messages to your friends, but you should never use them in any formal writing assignment.

Commonly Misspelled Words

achievement	*i* before *e* except after *c*
believe	*i* before *e* except after *c*
committee	2 *m*'s, 2 *t*'s, 2 *e*'s
definite	no *a*—just 2 *i*'s
occasion	2 *c*'s, but only one *s*
occurred	2 *c*'s, 2 *r*'s
parallel	There are 2 parallel *l*'s in the middle.
pleasant	There's an *-ant* in pleasant.
receive	*i* before *e* except after *c*
recommend	one *c*, 2 *m*'s
referring	only one f, two *r*'s
separate	There's *a rat* in separate

LEARNING TO PUNCTUATE

What's the point of punctuation? We'll show you. Take a look at these two sentences.

> Martha, my mother is the best pilot around.
> Martha, my mother, is the best pilot around.

In the first sentence, I am telling someone named Martha about my mother. In the second sentence, I am telling someone about my mother, whose name is Martha. The words in each sentence are exactly the same. The punctuation changes the meaning of the sentence.

Here's a sentence that could only have been written by an English teacher. Just for fun, can you find a way to punctuate it that will cause it to make sense?

> Finn where Jason had had had had had had had had had had had the teacher's approval.

Okay, here's the backstory. In this situation, two enthusiastic English students named Finn and Jason are arguing over whether a certain sentence should use the past tense *had* or the past perfect tense *had had*. Finn had argued for *had had*, and the teacher had said he was right. So...

> Finn, where Jason had had *had*, had had *had had*; *had had* had had the teacher's approval.

Try that sentence on your friends who think they know about punctuation!

With punctuation, certain rules may be open to interpretation, depending on your personal style. While you are learning, however, it's best not to fool around too much with long, strange, overly punctuated sentences. Keeping sentences relatively short and simple will keep you out of the punctuation mud for now. As you get more adventurous and confident, you can try your hand at interesting sentences filled with dashes, semicolons, and commas.

THE PERIOD

Use a period in the following instances:

1. When you are coming to a complete stop after a statement or a command.

   > The garden around my house is very dense. Elvis Presley was the greatest performer ever.

2. After most abbreviations. Monograms, government organizations, post office state abbreviations, and television and radio networks don't need periods. If you have an abbreviation at the end of a sentence, you only need one period. Look at the examples on the following page.

Mr. Panda
V.P. Cheney
etc.
A.M.
CBS
WBCI
KZOO
FBI
JFK

3. Inside parentheses, if they contain a complete sentence. Put the period outside the parentheses if the words inside do not make a complete sentence.

> (Lucy told him.)
> Lucy told him (not us).

4. Inside quotation marks at the end of a sentence.

> The sign said "Authorized Personnel Only."

THE COMMA

Use a comma in the following instances:

1. To separate two independent clauses connected by *and*, *but*, *or*, *nor*, or *for*.

Pierre was usually a good runner, but today he lost the race.
Tom was a good cook, and he always enjoyed eating what he made.

If the clauses are short enough, you may leave out the comma.

Manuel won and he was happy.
Tom cooked and ate the fish.

2. To separate items in a list. You should also put a comma before the last *and*.

I wanted to buy the new CD's by 50 Cent, U2, and the Tokyo String Quartet.

3. To set off an introductory phrase from the main sentence.

After eating 52 lemon pies, Billy had quite a bad stomachache.
Before leaving the party, Billy had to take some Alka-Seltzer.

4. To separate a list of adjectives if you could use *and* between them.

The fat, sickly, ugly, smelly baboon was sitting in the corner. (You could say, "The fat and sickly and ugly and smelly baboon...")

5. To separate the name of a person you are addressing, or a person's title.

> That is why, Mr. Dithers, Dagwood won't be at work today.
> Mr. Dithers, Dagwood's boss, is quite upset about the budget.

6. To set off a group of words that contrasts with what you are saying.

> I like to swim, not dive, when I go to the pool.
> Alice was going to sing, not dance, at the talent show.

7. To set apart the figures in a date and the parts of an address (however, not between the state and the zip code).

> July 4, 1776
> 35 Elm Street, Cleveland, OH 00001

8. To separate hundreds, thousands, millions, and every successive third digit thereafter.

> 1,876,967,300

9. To avoid confusion in a sentence. That's the main purpose of a comma, after all. If you need to pause, or set aside a group of words to make your meaning clear, use a comma. Try not to overdo it. The next sentence is confusing without a comma.

After waking up my sister ate breakfast.
Here's how it should read:
After waking up, my sister ate breakfast.

THE QUESTION MARK

Use a question mark as follows:

1. To show that a direct question is being asked.

    Do you want to go to The Bagel Emporium
    with me?

You don't need a question mark for an indirect question.

    She wanted to know if he would be going to
    the pet store with her.

2. Put the question mark inside quotation marks
    if the quotation is a question. Put the question
    mark outside the quotation marks if the quote
    itself is not a question.

    "Would you like some of this fish?"
    (The quoted sentence is a question.)

    Do you know who said, "Give me liberty or
    give me death"?
    (The quoted sentence is not a question.)

THE EXCLAMATION POINT

Use an exclamation point as follows:

1. If you are expressing a strong statement or sentiment.

    I really love that movie!

2. To set off an interjection for emphasis.

    Yikes! That fire is hot.

But don't overuse exclamation points. You'll seldom need them for the writing you do for school. People use them way too much. Try to limit the use of exclamation points to strong feelings and statements or your writing will look silly. Take a look at these two examples.

> **The Pineview Eagles have been having their best year ever! Star quarterback David Barzinski did a great job this past Saturday! He scored two touchdowns! It was a great game! Go, Eagles!**

This is much better:

> **The Pineview Eagles have been having their best year ever. Star quarterback David Barzinski did a great job this past Saturday. He scored two touchdowns. It was a great game. Go, Eagles!**

The first example seems as if the writer is yelling. It also loses its effectiveness after a while. Try to keep your use of exclamation points to a minimum, and never use two or more in the same place.

THE SEMICOLON

Semicolons are tricky, and many people use them incorrectly. Here are the rules.

1. Use a semicolon when two independent clauses are not joined by a conjunction. If you can separate the parts into two separate sentences, use a semicolon.

    > **Sharon thought that the fish was overcooked; the dinner was wonderful other than that. The results came in; the crowd couldn't wait to hear them announced.**

2. Use a semicolon if you have a long list of names that already includes commas. In this case, commas would not clearly separate the names, so use semicolons instead.

    > **We were soon joined by Prof. Elizabeth Young-Smith, head of the English department, from Middle Valley, Ohio; Dean Jane Farfetch, team leader, from West Hills, Indiana; and Ms. Petra Mustang, social studies teacher, from South Eastville, Michigan.**

Uses of a Period

The acronym SAD represents the three main uses of a period.

Use a period at the end of a sentence.

Use a period following an abbreviation. (Dr., Oct., or Mrs.)

Use a period as a decimal point. (99.9% or $57.25)

As you read this page, stomp your foot every time you come to a period that ends a sentence. Then, pick up any book or magazine, and do the same thing. This will emphasize the primary function of a period, which is creating pauses, or breaks, in a text.

THE COLON

A colon is used as follows:

1. To introduce a list.

    > The problems were always the same on the island: floods, volcanoes, and monsoons.

2. To introduce a long quote.

    > It was John F. Kennedy who said, "Ask not what your country can do for you; ask what you can do for your country."

3. To introduce an explanation.

    > There are many reasons for our coming here: we wanted to meet A.J., and we were interested in purchasing a new DVD player.

THE QUOTATION MARKS

Use quotation marks as follows:

1. Around a direct quotation. Put any commas or periods inside the quotation marks, regardless of the logic involved. Question marks and exclamation marks are used more

logically. They should be inside the quotation marks if they are part of the quotation and outside if they are not.

> "Let's get going," said Klara, "or we'll be late."
> "Don't you want to go?" asked Chris.
> "Look at me!" cried Roddy.
> I don't think Dr. Smith is aware that we call him "Dr. Know"!

2. To set off a statement that is the opposite of what you really mean. Only use quotation marks this way if it is absolutely necessary, or your writing will look silly.

> Michelle "borrowed" my homework so that she could copy it.

3. If a quotation is longer than one paragraph. Use new quotation marks at the beginning of each new paragraph, but only at the end of the last paragraph.

> "I went to the beach one day this summer. It was quite beautiful and sunny. The day was really picture perfect.
> "Then, to my surprise, a giant thundercloud passed over the sun. It began to rain. The day was completely ruined."

However, there is one exception to the quotation marks rule.

Exception: You don't need quotation marks for an indirect quotation.

> He told us that he would be happy to join us at the party. She said thank you to all her guests.

THE DASH

Dashes are optional. Some people like to use dashes, others don't. An occasional use can be effective, but don't overdo it. Dashes are used as follows:

1. You can use dashes like commas, to set off a phrase.

> She was quite a sight—all done up and wearing that new dress—for her sweet sixteen party.

2. To substitute dashes for parentheses.

> When you come to the party—it's going to be crowded—bring lots of tortilla chips and guacamole.

Instead of

> When you come to the party (it's going to be crowded), bring lots of tortilla chips and guacamole.

PARENTHESES

Parentheses are used to set off any extra words that would otherwise interrupt your sentence.

> Max (wonder-dog extraordinaire) was performing at the local talent show.

Punctuate the following passage. Remember that there is some flexibility here, but do your best and try to keep the passage clear. Rewrite the passage in the space provided after it.

Home Again

Our Greek wanderer Odysseus spent ten years fighting in Troy and he also survived ten years of adventures trying to get back to Ithaca from Troy which is in modern-day Turkey The attempt to get home involved scary enemies such as these jagged rocks a whirlpool a shipwreck and beautiful mermaids who hoped to make him forget about home

Finally he arrives back in Ithaca Hoping to check out things in the kingdom before he reveals his identity he disguises himself as a poor man a wanderer Also of course he is 20 years older

Do you think this disguise will work It isn't perfect as we'll see.

Amazingly enough or not Odysseus is first recognized by his dog This dog has not seen his master for 20 years but his special doggy talents allow him to see through the disguise Homer makes the dog seem very real giving him a name Argus and informing us that he suffers from fleas Odysseus is filled with emotion at seeing Argus but he must not reveal his feelings

In a second emotional scene Odysseus's old nurse who had tended to him as a child recognizes him While offering him traditional hospitality she recognizes a scar that he got as a boy. A fierce boar had gouged him with its tusks. The astonished nurse does not know whether to call him dear child or my master

I beg you dear nurse he whispers to her do not tell the others who I am

Dear boy I will keep your secret she replies but like Argus she is filled with emotion

Some of the final scenes are violent but the reader is most touched by Odysseus's reunion with Penelope Although his wife has been faithful to him for his 20 years' absence she is a match for her husband in courage and cunning. To get him to prove his identity she tells a lie about the very special bed he long ago built for the two of them You must read Book 23 of *The Odyssey* to learn about this bed her lie and his response

Ultimately though we may imagine Odysseus uttering the famous sentiment There's no place like home

CHAPTER 9

Cool Books for Cool Readers

Reading is a surefire way to improve your grammar and your vocabulary. But reading stories, novels, and poetry has even more benefits than the help it gives to your sense of the English language. You can read for entertainment and for escape. You can read to gain factual knowledge or to extend your range of emotional perception. You can find out about the lives of young people who have grown up in places, cultures, or time periods different from your own, or you can learn about great women and men of all eras. The wonderful poet Emily Dickinson once said there was no ship like a book to take you on a wonderful journey. (Notice that there are no quotation marks around that last sentence—it's not a direct quotation!) We might update Dickinson's image and say reading is like going on a trip, but without the delays or the long security lines at the airport.

The following list includes books recommended by teachers, librarians, and—most important—other young people. We think you may really enjoy them! Check out the books in your library (get the pun?) and take home the ones that seem interesting to you. If you like a book, you can ask your parents, friends, teacher, or librarian to recommend others like it. But if you're not hooked after you've read a few chapters of a book, don't worry about it. Try something else. Nobody's grading you!

So, as we end this book, we encourage you to keep thinking about language and the interesting effects you can create through the way you use words. (Remember, we told you earlier that the word *glamour* comes from the word *grammar*!) Keep reading, writing, and building your vocabulary. Gaining power over language is one of the coolest things you can do.

COOL BOOKS FOR COOL READERS

▶ Adams, Douglas. *The Hitchhiker's Guide to the Galaxy.* (Science Fiction, Humor)

The first book in a series that includes *The Restaurant at the End of the Universe; Life, the Universe & Everything; So Long and Thanks for All the Fish;* and *Mostly Harmless.*

▶ Alcott, Louisa May. *Little Women.* (Classic)

This classic story of four sisters growing up during the American Civil War has several movie versions.

▶ Babbitt, Natalie. *Tuck Everlasting.* (Fantasy)

A story about a family who finds the fountain of youth. Babbitt's other books include *The Eyes of the Amaryllis* and *Kneeknock Rise.*

▶ Block, Francesca Lia. *Weetzie Bat.* (Contemporary Fiction)

The first book in a series, which has also been published in the volume *Dangerous Angels: The Weetzie Bat Books.*

▶ Blume, Judy. *Tiger Eyes.* (Contemporary Fiction)

Blume has written many other popular books for young people, including *Blubber* and *Just as Long as We're Together.*

▶ Carroll, Lewis. *Alice's Adventures in Wonderland.* (Classic)

Alice's adventures continue in *Through the Looking Glass.*

▶ Cooper, Susan. *The Dark Is Rising.* (Fantasy)

The first book in a series that includes *Greenwitch, The Grey King,* and *Silver on the Tree. Over Sea, Under Stone* is the prequel to this series.

▶ Cormier, Robert. *The Chocolate War.* (Contemporary Fiction)

Once heavily censored, *The Chocolate War* tells the story of one young boy's efforts to challenge the cultural norms enforced by his school's mob rule.

▶ Creech, Sharon. *Walk Two Moons.* (Contemporary Fiction)

Creech has written other novels for young people, including *Chasing Redbird* and *The Wanderer.*

▶ Curtis, Christopher Paul. *Bud, Not Buddy.* (Contemporary Fiction)

A 10-year old boy crosses the country to find a man who just might be his long-lost father.

▶ DiCamillo, Kate. *Because of Winn-Dixie.* (Contemporary Fiction)

Some other popular books by DiCamillo are *The Tiger Rising* and *The Miraculous Journey of Edward Tulane.*

▶ Dorris, Michael. *The Window.* (Contemporary Fiction)

Dorris also wrote about the main character of this novel, Rayona, in his first novel, *A Yellow Raft in Blue Water.*

▶ Fitzgerald, John D. *The Great Brain.* (Historical Fiction)

The first book in a series that includes *More Adventures of the Great Brain, Me and My Little Brain, The Great Brain at the Academy, The Great Brain Reforms, The Return of the Great Brain, The Great Brain Does It Again,* and *The Great Brain Is Back.*

▶ George, Jean Craighead. *Julie of the Wolves.* (Contemporary Fiction)

George has written two other books about Julie, *Julie* and *Julie's Wolf Pack,* as well as *My Side of the Mountain.*

▶ Hinton, S. E. *The Outsiders.* (Contemporary Fiction)

S. E. Hinton wrote this novel when she was a high school junior.

▶ Hughes, Langston. *The Dream Keeper and Other Poems.* (Poetry)

A collection of poems by this legendary African American poet.

▶ Juster, Norton. *The Phantom Tollbooth.* (Fantasy, Humor)

A classic book about a bored little boy who finds a strange tollbooth in his bedroom and drives his toy car through it and into another world.

▶ Konigsburg, E. L. *From the Mixed-Up Files of Mrs. Basil E. Frankweiler.* (Contemporary Fiction)

The story of a precocious girl who decides to run away from her parents and take up residence at the Metropolitan Museum of Art.

▶ Lee, Gus. *China Boy.* (Contemporary Fiction)
Also read the sequel, *Honor and Duty.*

▶ LeGuin, Ursula. *A Wizard of Earthsea.* (Fantasy)
The first book in a series that also includes *The Tombs of Atuan, The Farthest Shore,* and *Tehanu.*

▶ L'Engle, Madeleine. *A Wrinkle in Time.* (Science Fiction, Contemporary Fiction)
L'Engle's series about the Murry family continues in *A Swiftly Tilting Planet, A Wind in the Door, An Acceptable Time,* and *Many Waters.* Also try *A Ring of Endless Light,* a favorite in her series about Vicky Austin and her family.

▶ Lewis, C. S. *The Lion, the Witch, and the Wardrobe.* (Classic, Fantasy)
The first book in *The Chronicles of Narnia.*

▶ Lowry, Lois. *The Giver.* (Soft Science Fiction)
Eleven-year-old Jonas lives in a perfect world, one where there is no sadness, no pain, and no suffering. But when he turns 12, he finds out that maybe his world isn't so perfect after all.

▶ Montgomery, L.M. *Anne of Green Gables.* (Classic)
Anne Shirley's story continues in *Anne of Avonlea* and *Anne of the Island. Rainbow Valley* and *Rilla of Ingleside* are about her children. Also try Montgomery's series about Emily Starr: *Emily of New Moon, Emily Climbs,* and *Emily's Quest.*

▶ Myers, Walter Dean. *Hoops.* (Contemporary Fiction)
Myers has written dozens of books, including *Fallen Angels* and *Monster.*

▶ Nye, Naomi Shihab. *Habibi*. (Contemporary Fiction)

The autobiographical story of an Arab-American teenager who moves to Jerusalem in the 1970s.

▶ O'Dell, Scott. *Island of the Blue Dolphins*. (Contemporary Fiction)

Other books by O'Dell include *The Black Pearl* and *Sing Down the Moon*.

▶ Park, Linda Sue. *A Single Shard*. (Contemporary Fiction)

Park's other books include *Project Mulberry* and *The Kite Fighters*.

▶ Paterson, Katherine. *Bridge to Terabithia*. (Contemporary Fiction)

Other popular books by Paterson include The Great Gilly Hopkins, The Master Puppeteer, and Jacob Have I Loved.

▶ Paulsen, Gary. *Nightjohn*. (Historical Fiction)

Paulsen3 has also written a sequel, *Sarny*, as well as many adventure books, including *Hatchet*, the first in a series.

▶ Pullman, Philip. The *His Dark Materials* trilogy. (Fantasy that reads like reality)

The separate volumes are *The Golden Compass*, *The Subtle Knife*, and *The Amber Spyglass*. Some readers like these books even better than the Harry Potter volumes!

▶ Rawls, Wilson. *Where the Red Fern Grows*. (Classic)

Adventure story about a boy who acquires and trains two hunting dogs.

▶ Rowling, J. K. *Harry Potter and the Sorcerer's Stone.* (Fantasy)

The first book in a wildly popular series that includes *Harry Potter and the Chamber of Secrets, Harry Potter and the Prisoner of Azkaban, Harry Potter and the Goblet of Fire, Harry Potter and the Order of the Phoenix, Harry Potter and the Half-Blood Prince.* The series ended with the seventh book, *Harry Potter and the Deathly Hallows.*

▶ Salinger, J. D. *The Catcher in the Rye.* (Classic)

If you don't like the first paragraph of this book, it means you should wait a few more years before you read it. It's great, but only if you're ready for it.

▶ de Saint-Exupery, Antoine. *The Little Prince.* (Classic, Fantasy)

The essence of this book is contained in the famous line uttered by the fox to the Little Prince: "It is only with the heart that one can see rightly; what is essential is invisible to the eye."

▶ Smith, Betty. *A Tree Grows in Brooklyn.* (Classic)

A wonderful growing-up story set in early-twentieth-century New York.

▶ Soto, Gary. *Baseball in April and Other Stories.* (Contemporary Fiction)

Also try Soto's novel, *Crazy Weekend,* and *Neighborhood Odes,* a collection of his poetry.

▶ Spinelli, Jerry. *Maniac Magee.* (Contemporary Fiction)

Other books by Spinelli include *Loser, Crash*, and *Love, Stargirl.*

▶ Staples, Suzanne Fisher. *Shabanu: Daughter of the Wind.* (Contemporary Fiction)

Shabanu's story continues in *Haveli.*

► Stevenson, Robert Louis. *Treasure Island* (Classic)

Although almost all the characters are male, plenty of girls—as well as boys—have enjoyed reading it.

► Taylor, Mildred D. *Roll of Thunder, Hear My Cry.* (Historical Fiction)

The story of an African American family living in rural Mississippi during the 1930s.

► Tolkien, J. R. R. *The Hobbit.* (Fantasy)

The prequel to *The Lord of the Rings* series, which includes *The Fellowship of the Ring, The Two Towers,* and *The Return of the King.*

► Voigt, Cynthia. *Homecoming.* (Contemporary Fiction)

The first book about Dicey Tillerman's family and friends; others include *Dicey's Song, A Solitary Blue,* and *Seventeen Against the Dealer.*

► Wojciechowska, Maia. *Shadow of a Bull.* (Fiction)

The story of a young boy training to follow in his matador father's footsteps while secretly yearning to follow his dream to become a doctor.

► Yep, Laurence. *Dragonwings.* (Historical Fiction)

Also try Yep's other novels about Chinese-American life, *Child of the Owl* and *Dragon's Gate.*

► Zindel, Paul. *The Pigman.* (Contemporary Fiction)

The story of two high school students whose lives change when they meet an eccentric old man they nickname "The Pigman."

GLOSSARY

active voice: when the subject performs the action described by the verb (as compared to the passive voice, when the action described by the verb happens to the subject) (*Charisse drove to the store.*)

adjective: a word that describes a noun or a pronoun (*beautiful, smart, nice, happy*)

adverb: a word that describes a verb, an adjective, or another adverb. Adverbs often, but do not always, end in *-ly* (*quickly, very, nicely*)

agreement: a term used either to indicate that the subject must agree with the verb (*he smiles* instead of *he smile*) or that the pronoun must agree with the noun it replaces (*The people want their hamburgers* instead of *The people want his hamburger.*)

appositive: a phrase (usually a noun), set off by commas, that explains something (John, *my best friend,* is getting me tickets to the concert.)

apostrophe: a punctuation mark that shows ownership (*Mark's bicycle*) or a contraction (*don't, won't*) to show that the letters have been left out

article: a special group of adjectives that refer to people, places, ideas, or things. *The, a,* and *an* are articles.

case: form that shows the function of a pronoun. The subjective (or nominative) case pronoun is used in the *subject* of a sentence. The objective case is used in the *object* of a sentence

clause: a group of words with a subject and a verb. Independent clauses may stand alone; dependent clauses may not

collective noun: a group noun that is usually treated as singular in number (*audience, jury, government*)

colon: a punctuation mark used to introduce a list or an example and to separate the hours and minutes in the time of day (*We need two things: courage and patience.*)

comma: a punctuation mark used for a pause, or to set off part of a sentence for clarity

conjunction: a joining word that may act alone or in pairs. *And, but,* and *or* are conjunctions that act alone. *Neither... nor, either... or,* and *not only... but* are conjunctions that work in pairs

dash: a punctuation mark that may be used like a comma or parentheses (*You know—don't you—that I really like to skate.*)

demonstrative pronoun: a pronoun used to point out specific people, places, things, or ideas (*that, these, those, this*)

dependent clause: a group of words with a subject and a verb that would not make sense standing alone as a sentence (*When the boy cried,* his mother came running.)

diction: correct word choice

direct object: the noun that receives the action of the verb in the sentence (I want to eat *hamburgers.*)

future tense: a verb tense used to indicate an action that will happen. Uses the words *will* or *shall*

future perfect tense: a verb tense used to show an action that will be finished before a specific time in the future (Before next Wednesday, I *will have lost* five pounds.)

gender: applies to nouns and pronouns that refer to people. It can either be male, female, or neutral (applying to both men and women)

gerund: *-ing* form of a verb, which acts as a noun (*Skating* is great.)

helping verb: words used with the main verb to form tenses (We *will* go to the park. I *have been* trying not to eat ice cream.)

idiom: a phrase that doesn't make sense literally or follow any specific grammar rule. Idioms include funny expressions (*Let a smile be your umbrella.*) and preposition use (*A foot is different from a meter.*)

indefinite pronoun: a pronoun that doesn't stand for a particular noun. *Each, either, any, few, none,* and *some* are indefinite pronouns.

independent clause: the main clause of a sentence. It can stand alone, without the dependent clauses (When the boy cried, *his mother came running.*)

indirect object: the receiver of the direct object (Give *me* your skates.) that can be turned into a prepositional phrase (Give your skates *to me.*)

infinitive: the *to* form of the verb (*to be, to go, to eat*) that is used as a noun, adjective, or adverb

interjection: a word used for emphasis (*Cool! Yikes! Wow! Hey!*)

interrogative pronoun: a pronoun used to ask a question (*Who? What? Which?*)

misplaced modifier: a phrase or word that is not next to the thing it is modifying. It usually makes a sentence unclear

modify: to describe. Adjectives and adverbs are modifiers

nominative case: also called *subjective case.* The pronoun used if it is the subject of a verb

noun: a person, place, thing, or idea (*bookworm, Denver, house, truth*)

number: term describing whether something is singular or plural.

object: the object of a verb is the thing acted upon by the subject. (I ate *ice cream.*) The *object of a preposition* is the noun that is being placed by the preposition (We went to *the house.*)

objective case: the form of pronoun that is used as the object of a verb

parallel construction: the rule that when you construct a list, all the things in the list should be in the same form

participle: a verb form that acts as an adjective (Katie couldn't deal with the *annoying* sounds.)

past tense: the verb tense that indicates that something has already happened.

past perfect: the verb tense describing past before the past (Before I went to the dance, I *had gone* to the store.)

period: punctuation mark used at the end of a statement or in abbreviations

person: the term used to categorize personal pronouns. *First person* refers to the speaker: I, we. *Second person* refers to the person being spoken to: you. *Third person* refers to the person being spoken about: he, she, they

phrase: a group of words that work together as one part of speech in a sentence. The main types of phrases are *prepositional, infinitive, participial,* and *gerund.*

plural: more than one, as opposed to *singular.* Nouns, pronouns, and verbs may be plural or singular

possessive pronoun: pronoun that shows ownership (*my, his, hers, its, theirs*)

predicate: the part of the sentence that includes the verb and all words related to it

preposition: a word used to place a noun in time or space (*at, toward, around, before, into, after*)

present tense: verb tense used to show that something is happening right now or to state a fact

present perfect: verb tense used to show an action that began in the past but continues into the present, or was finished at some indefinite, earlier time (I *have lost* fifteen pounds.)

principal parts: the basic forms of the verb that are used for the different tenses. The principal parts include the *present, past,* and *past participle*

pronoun: a word that stands in for a noun (*he, she, it, they*)

question mark: a punctuation mark used at the end of a question (*How are you?*)

quotation mark: punctuation marks used to set off a quote or the title of certain works (*"How are you?" asked Jennifer.*)

redundancy: saying the same thing twice; using unnecessary words

reflexive pronoun: pronoun that refers to the subject (*He ate it himself.*) It can also be used for emphasis (*I, myself, am outraged.*)

semicolon: a punctuation mark used to separate independent clauses in a compound sentence (*I came; I saw; I conquered.*)

singular: refers to nouns and pronouns when there is only one, as opposed to two or more. Singular is also used to refer to the verb that goes with a singular noun or pronoun

subject: the noun or pronoun that performs the action in a sentence. Sometimes, it includes descriptive words that come before the noun or pronoun

tense: the form of a verb that tells when an action happened. The six main tenses are *present, present perfect, past, past perfect, future*, and *future perfect.*

verb: a word that expresses an action or a state of being. You must have a verb to have a sentence (*run, jump, seem, think*)

verbal: a phrase that contains a verb and any modifiers that doesn't act like a verb. The three main types of verbals are *gerunds, infinitives*, and *participles*

ANSWERS

The proper nouns that you were asked to circle are in boldface here.

Zeus, the <u>leader</u> of the Greek <u>gods</u>, was sitting on his ebony <u>throne</u> at the <u>top</u> of **Mt. Olympus**. In his <u>hand</u> he was holding a jagged <u>thunderbolt</u>, which made him look powerful. But the <u>truth</u> is that he was feeling a little lonely and wanted some <u>companionship</u>, so he called for his <u>brother</u>.

"Yo, **Poseidon**!" he called in an ungodlike <u>way</u>. "Are you still the <u>king</u> of the <u>sea</u>?"

"Oh, <u>brother</u>," said **Poseidon**. "You know it's a lifetime <u>position</u>. I wear <u>seaweed</u> in my <u>hair</u>. The <u>mermaids</u> are my royal <u>subjects</u>. I sleep with the <u>fishes</u>."

"Just checking," said the <u>king</u> of the <u>gods</u>, adjusting the <u>angle</u> of his <u>thunderbolt</u> toward southern **Greece**. "Where's the <u>goddess</u> of <u>love</u>?"

Aphrodite glided forward in a <u>chariot</u> pulled by <u>peacocks</u>. "The <u>world</u> of <u>romance</u> is getting ready for **Valentine's Day**, although it's not until mid-**February**. I'm teaching **Cupid** to cut <u>hearts</u> out of red <u>paper</u>, but he keeps trying to do it with his <u>blindfold</u> on. That <u>boy</u>!"

"Hmm, **Valentine's Day**," mused Zeus quietly. "That reminds me. I know my <u>wife</u>'s <u>birthday</u> is soon. I'd better start thinking of a <u>gift</u> for **Hera**. Last <u>year</u> I forgot, and she threw a Grecian <u>urn</u> at me."

Answers are underlined. (Note: Possessive personal pronouns are often treated as adjectives, but they are included in the answer key.)

Zeus came out of <u>his</u> trance of thinking about Hera's birthday. <u>He</u> saw Poseidon looking at <u>his</u> wristwatch. Aphrodite looked as if <u>she</u> were impatient. "<u>They</u> are waiting for <u>me</u> to speak," <u>he</u> realized.

"Okay," Zeus said briskly. "<u>We</u> need to think hard. Does Hera need an iPod? Would <u>she</u> prefer more perfume? <u>I</u> know <u>she</u> likes frangipani. This gift for <u>her</u>—where can <u>I</u> buy <u>it</u>?"

Aphrodite smiled sweetly at <u>him</u>. "Why don't <u>I</u> have <u>my</u> husband Hephaestus make <u>her</u> a sculpture of some kind? <u>He</u> is a divine blacksmith, <u>you</u> know, and <u>he</u> has made some nifty things. <u>She</u>'ll be grateful to <u>me</u>...<u>I</u> mean to <u>us</u>...for this idea."

Poseidon looked at <u>them</u>. "No, too arty. <u>I</u> think good old-fashioned roses would be better for <u>her</u>. Let<u>'s</u> get

Hermes to deliver <u>them</u>. After all, <u>he</u> has wings on <u>his</u> hat and on <u>his</u> shoes!"

QUIZ #3: VERBS

Answers are underlined.

Hermes <u>flew</u> toward the throne of Zeus and <u>landed</u> with an abrupt jolt. He <u>removed</u> his hat with the wings and <u>tucked</u> it under his arm.

"I <u>am</u> at your service, Zeus. I <u>will</u> <u>do</u> your bidding," he <u>said</u> with a polite semi-bow.

"Greetings, Hermes. You <u>will</u> <u>deliver</u> my birthday gift to my wife, Hera. I <u>expect</u> your full cooperation. You <u>should</u> <u>fly</u> with the speed of lightning," he <u>said</u> as he <u>crinkled</u> his eyebrows in a way that <u>gave</u> him a look of even greater importance.

Hermes <u>wondered</u> why Zeus <u>questioned</u> his speed. After all, he too <u>was</u> a god, not just a flunky who <u>delivered</u> packages. But still it <u>was</u> true that Zeus <u>was</u> more powerful, so he <u>muttered</u> only, "But of course."

"Please <u>see</u> to it that the gift <u>is</u> <u>wrapped</u> in the highest-quality papyrus from the banks of the Nile," <u>said</u> Zeus. "And do not <u>rattle,</u> <u>shake,</u> or <u>drop</u> the box as you <u>are</u> <u>carrying</u> it. <u>Is</u> this clear?"

"Of course. <u>Give</u> me the gift and I <u>will</u> <u>fulfill</u> your commands."

"The gift? Oh, yes. I <u>have</u> <u>decided</u> that flowers <u>are</u> too ordinary, but I <u>have</u> confidence you <u>will</u> <u>think</u> of something."

Answers are underlined. (Note: Possessive nouns and pronouns are treated here as adjectives.)

Hermes marveled at <u>Zeus's</u> <u>cocky</u> manner. Why should the <u>delivery</u> god have to decide on the <u>perfect</u> gift? He knew he needed <u>wise</u> advice, so why not go to Athena, the supremely <u>wise</u> goddess of wisdom?

He found her in <u>her</u> <u>cavernous</u> chamber, sitting in front of a <u>large</u> loom. In addition to <u>her</u> <u>great</u> wisdom, Athena was a <u>super-duper</u> weaver, and had once won an <u>important</u> <u>weaving</u> competition with Arachne. Hermes chuckled as he recalled how Athena had transformed Arachne into a <u>big</u>, <u>hairy</u> spider after the contest. He would be very <u>polite</u> to Athena.

"Oh, <u>divine</u> Athena," he began, as he entered the <u>huge</u> room. "Your <u>superior</u> wisdom is needed. What should Zeus give the <u>picky</u> Hera for <u>her</u> birthday?"

Answers are underlined.

"Zeus <u>always</u> gets other gods to do his work!" said Athena <u>crossly</u>. "Can he <u>never</u> think of anything but himself? <u>Although</u> I am <u>very</u> wise, this is a waste of my wisdom."

Hermes paused and <u>then</u> spoke <u>flatteringly</u>. "I could <u>never</u> be as wise as you. I tried <u>once</u>, but it was impossible."

Athena smiled <u>sweetly</u>, for compliments <u>always</u> pleased her. "Let's see. <u>Maybe</u> I can think of something. Hera is <u>quite</u> vain, I believe. Vain women like her <u>never</u> tire of looking at themselves. Get Hephaestus to cut a round piece of bronze and polish it <u>vigorously</u>. Hera will <u>then</u> be able to see her reflection without having to trek to the royal reflecting pool. <u>Carefully</u> place a gold ornament of an eagle at the top and the bottom. Hera will <u>then</u> be <u>immensely</u> pleased. <u>Now</u>, what shall we call my brilliant new invention?"

Hermes <u>modestly</u> bowed his head in tribute to her genius. "Looking glass," he said <u>quietly</u>. "Looking glass. That's it!"

Answers are underlined.

Hephaestus limped slowly <u>toward</u> his furnace. Where was it? He reached <u>around</u> his workbench and patted the stone floor <u>under</u> it. There was his anvil, and <u>beside</u> it was his burlap sack <u>of</u> metals. He put his left hand <u>in</u> the bag and felt <u>for</u> a round object. He produced a perfect circle <u>of</u> bronze. <u>During</u> the next half hour he polished and polished <u>with</u> his godly rag. Then he looked <u>into</u> it and saw his own fire-reddened face. "Amazing!" he thought. "I'm not crazy <u>about</u> Hera, but this is a wonderful gift <u>for</u> her."

<u>Among</u> his other scraps <u>of</u> metal were fragments <u>of</u> silver and gold. <u>From</u> these he fashioned four small eagles and soldered them <u>onto</u> the edges <u>of</u> the bronze. This was indeed a gift worthy <u>of</u> a goddess. "I'm still glad I'm married <u>to</u> Aphrodite," he thought, "but Athena and I make a great professional team!"

Answers are underlined.

The lame <u>but</u> skilled blacksmith took his beautiful <u>and</u> useful creation <u>and</u> wrapped it in a cloth of purple velvet to prevent it from getting broken <u>or</u> cracked. He wanted to show it off, <u>but</u> he knew Zeus was taking a nap. For that matter, <u>neither</u> Aphrodite <u>nor</u> Hermes was around, <u>for</u> they both had made quick trips to earth. (Aphrodite was having her picture painted <u>while</u> she stood—nude!—on a large half-shell, <u>and</u> Hermes was giving endorsements to a scarf company in western Gaul <u>and</u> to his favorite sports team, the Trojan Horses.)

Was what happened next chance <u>or</u> fate? Hephaestus spotted <u>not only</u> Artemis, the goddess of hunting with her bow and arrow, <u>but also</u> her twin, Apollo, that versatile chap who was god of <u>both</u> music <u>and</u> healing.

Hephaestus shouted, "Look at my new invention!" <u>for</u> he was very proud of it.

Artemis set down her weapons <u>and</u> shushed the hound that accompanied her. "I love it!" she cried. "Can I have it? I can use it to look behind me when I hunt. Then no crafty boar <u>or</u> sly bear will be able to sneak up on me."

"Actually, Sister," said Apollo, "Hephaestus should give it—_or_ even sell it—to me. My chariot could use a rear-view looking glass."

"No way," said Hephaestus with certainty. "This is headed for Hera, the goddess-who-must-be-obeyed, _and_ for no one else."

QUIZ #8: INTERJECTIONS

Answers are underlined.

Wow! What a sight the Great Hall of Olympus was! Streamers of gold and silver (that's real gold and silver) festooned the room. All of the gods of Mt. Olympus had gathered for Hera's birthday party, and, _man_, were they having a good time! When they had finished playing Pin the Tail on the Centaur (_alas_, the blindfolded Cupid had almost pinned the tail on Hera herself) and had eaten their nectar-and-ambrosia birthday cake, Zeus was ready to hand over his birthday surprise—the first looking glass ever known to men (or gods).

Hermes, who was responsible for getting the present to the party, was panicking. "_Yikes_! Where did I put that package? _Oh no_! Did Apollo forget to return it after he examined it? _Eek_!" He glanced frantically around the Great Hall, furrowing his brow. <u>Aha</u>! There it was on the mantel over the great fireplace. "<u>Yes</u>!" he cried, pumping his fist in the air and handing the velvet-covered box to Zeus.

"By <u>Hercules</u>," muttered Zeus. "I was afraid you'd forgotten it." Then he kissed Hera on the cheek and said, "<u>Well</u>, <u>well</u>, I guess it's time for a little gift."

Hera pulled back the soft wrapping and saw the shining brass circle with its eagle ornamentation. "<u>Oh my</u>," she said, "this is beautiful!" And when she held it up to her face and realized it held her reflection, she shouted, "<u>Yippee</u>! Now I can admire my beauty whenever I like. You've made me very happy, Zeus."

Her husband thought, "<u>Zounds</u>! I've managed to please her. <u>Hip, hip, hooray</u> for the creative team of Athena and Hephaestus!"

CHAPTER 1 REVIEW

There are *eight* parts of speech. Can you name them? Give a quick definition and an example of each one.

1.   **noun:** names a person, place, thing, or idea
     book, story, love, justice, truth, cat, dog, fish

2. **pronoun:** takes the place of a noun
he, she, it, they, their, its, mine, myself

3. **verb:** describes action or state of being
run, dance, seem, appear, think, is, were

4. **adjective:** describes a noun or pronoun
ugly, pretty, nice, small, big

5. **adverb:** describes a verb, adjective, or another adverb
quickly, nicely, fast, very, so

6. **preposition:** relates a noun or pronoun to another word in a sentence; usually refers to time and space
after, before, in, to, out, from, over

7. **conjunction:** joins parts of a sentence
and, or, but

8. **interjection:** word used for emphasis
hah!, yikes!, cool!

Answers are underlined.

1. The <u>Romans</u> gave the name "Jupiter" to Zeus.

2. <u>Hera</u> was called "Juno" by them.

3. <u>You</u> can probably guess the Roman name of Aphrodite, goddess of love.

4. Her Roman <u>name</u> was Venus. Were <u>you</u> right?

5. Most <u>speakers</u> of English think of her as Venus.

QUIZ #10: COMPLETE SUBJECTS

Underline each verb and circle the complete subject that goes with it. (Note: Verbs are underlined and complete subjects are shown in italics.)

Ares, the god of war, <u>needed</u> some soldiers. He <u>wanted</u> more than a few good men—*this powerful god*

<u>wanted</u> several good men. *This god with the bronze helmet* <u>knew</u> about the future. There <u>would</u> <u>be</u> *a talented mortal with the name of Homer.* Someday, *this Homer* <u>would</u> <u>write</u> a great poem about Greek soldiers. *This poet with the sublime style* <u>would</u> <u>tell</u> of the Greeks' defeat of the Trojans in the Trojan War. *The Greek god of war* <u>wanted</u> the Greeks to look very brave and very clever in Homer's poem. *The current Greek army and its descendents in future years* <u>must</u> <u>be</u> very unusual fighters.

What <u>will</u> *this long poem of the future* <u>say</u> about the Greeks? *This poem of 24 books* <u>will</u> <u>show</u> their bravery and <u>will</u> also <u>show</u> their cleverness. *The Trojans and their ruler, King Priam,* <u>are</u> also very brave. But *these Trojans with their long spears* <u>lack</u> the outrageous cleverness of the Greeks. *This poem,* The Iliad, <u>must</u> <u>depict</u> the Greeks at their best. And so *a crafty man named Odysseus* is very interesting to the god of war on his quest.

QUIZ #11: THE PREDICATE

The complete subjects are underlined, and the complete predicates are noted by parentheses.

<u>Ares</u> (wanted this Greek named Odysseus for the army). (Should) <u>a powerful god of war</u> (have to do this

work for himself)? (In the early morning) <u>Ares</u> (appeared in a dream to the Greek general Menelaus).

"<u>You</u> (should go to the island of Ithaca)."

"(Why should) <u>I</u> (go there)? <u>I</u> (like Sparta)." <u>Menelaus</u> (had a lot on his mind).

"<u>You</u> (must find Odysseus and sign him up for the war). <u>I</u> (command it)."

<u>The</u> <u>Greek</u> <u>general</u> (knew he had no choice). <u>He</u> (did hope to get some personal benefits out of this trip). "<u>I</u> (need new horses and a chariot for the trip). <u>My</u> <u>old</u> <u>chariot</u> (is getting very rusty). (Can) <u>I</u> (have a matched pair of black horses?)" <u>Menelaus</u> (knew how to bargain, even with a god).

"<u>Two</u> <u>black</u> <u>horses</u> <u>and</u> <u>a</u> <u>new</u> <u>chariot</u> (are on their way to you). <u>I</u> (don't want any more excuses). <u>This</u> <u>trip</u> <u>to</u> <u>Ithaca</u> (will be a long one). [<u>You</u>] (start on your way)."

"<u>Your</u> <u>slightest</u> <u>wish</u> (is my command). <u>I</u> (will find Odysseus)."

Complete sentences are marked with an "S."
Fragments with an "F."

S	1.	Menelaus did go to Ithaca.
F	2.	Where he found Odysseus.
F	3.	Plowing his field with salt and pretending he was insane.
S	4.	Odysseuswashappywithhiswifeand young child.
F	5.	And didn't want to go off to war.
S	6.	Menelaus had to plan a trick.
F	7.	Whichhedid,assoonashethoughtof a good one.
S	8.	It's hard to trick a tricky man like Odysseus!
S	9.	Has history recorded Menelaus's actions?
F	10.	AtrickinvolvingOdysseus'sbabyson Telemachus.

Parentheses are around each prepositional phrase.

1. (In Ithaca) Odysseus was plowing the field (with a donkey).

2. Plowing should be done (with oxen), so using donkeys made him look insane.

3. Also, farmers (in their right minds) plant seeds.

4. Odysseus was planting salt (in his fields).

5. But Menelaus set the baby Telemachus (in the path) (of Odysseus's plow).

6. The loving father instantly swerved the plow (away from his son).

7. (To Menelaus), this action proved he was not a raving madman.

8. Odysseus was now headed (for the Trojan War) and would not see his son (for twenty years).

Dependent clauses are underlined and parentheses are around the independent clauses.

1. <u>During the Trojan War</u>, (Odysseus showed his own trickiness).

2. <u>Unless you have read Homer's poetry,</u> (you may not know about his biggest trick).

3. (He dreamed up the idea of the giant artificial horse) <u>where soldiers could hide</u>.

4. <u>Before they realized the trick,</u> (the Trojans had pulled the beautiful Trojan Horse inside their city walls).

5. (They were horrified) <u>when, during the dark night, several soldiers crawled out of the belly of the horse</u>!

**Sample compound or complex sentences are
below. There is more than one correct way to
rewrite each.**

1. The soldiers came out of the horse. The Trojans were shocked.
   When the soldiers came out of the horse, the Trojans were shocked.

2. The soldiers headed for the palace. They set many fires.
   The soldiers headed for the palace, where they set many fires.

3. The sleepy Trojans wanted to stop them. They weren't organized enough.
   The sleepy Trojans wanted to stop them, but they weren't organized enough.

4. The soldiers got to the palace. It was located at the top of the hill.
   The soldiers got to the palace, which was located at the top of the hill.

5. Priam, the king of Troy, tried to defend himself. He was too old.
   Priam, the king of Troy, tried to defend himself, but he was too old.

6. Priam died bravely. Later, his brave son Hector had to face the fiercest Greek soldier, Achilles.

   Priam died bravely, but later, his brave son Hector had to face the fiercest Greek soldier, Achilles.

   OR

   Although Priam died bravely, later his brave son Hector had to face the fiercest Greek soldier, Achilles.

7. We know Hector was also a family man. He loved his wife, Andromache, and their baby son.

   We know Hector was also a family man who loved his wife, Andromache, and their baby son.

8. Hector's son was frightened by the plume on his father's helmet. Hector removed the helmet.

   When Hector's son was frightened by the plume on his father's helmet, Hector removed the helmet.

Sample simple sentences are below.

(There is more than one correct way to re-write each.)

9. The Trojan War began when a prince from Troy whose name was Paris took Helen away from Sparta.

The Trojan War began when Paris, a prince from Troy, took Helen away from Sparta.

10. You may find it odd that Helen, who was from Greece, is now called Helen of Troy.
You may find it odd that the Greek Helen is now called Helen of Troy.

QUIZ #16: PUTTING IT ALL TOGETHER

In the following sentences, the verbs of the main clauses are italicized and the simple subjects are underlined. Also, each sentence is marked "S" if it is a simple sentence, "C" if it is a compound sentence, and "X" if it is a complex sentence.

X 1. Hector *had to face* Achilles, who was the fiercest of the Greeks.

S 2. He *needed* help!

S 3. But no help was powerful enough to save him from the fierce Achilles.

X 4. Achilles was especially savage at this time because his best friend had been killed in the war.

__X__ 5. Although his friend had worn Achilles's armor, he had still been killed.

__C__ 6. Achilles *thirsted* for revenge, and <u>Hector</u> *was* there at just the wrong moment.

__S__ 7. What a sad event their hand-to-hand <u>battle</u> *was*!

__C__ 8. Later, <u>Priam</u> humbly *went* to see Achilles, and <u>he</u> *was* able to take his son's body home for a proper funeral.

__X__ 9. Hector's funeral <u>rites</u> *lasted* for several days because he had been such an important Trojan warrior.

QUIZ #17: SINGULAR AND PLURAL NOUNS

The plural nouns are in parentheses.

1. The Greek warriors never ate (bananas).

2. Did King Agamemnon have any pet (monkeys)?

3. No, his throne was flanked by two (cheetahs), whose (feet) had extra-long (claws).

4. He had special (boxes) made for these (creatures) whose (names) were Agatha and Pantho.

5. Each box had two (shelves) to hold the spare (collars) of the beasts.

6. (Workmen) used (knives) made of volcanic lava to craft the scalloped (edges) of each box.

7. The bronze for the (boxes) had to be heated to very high (temperatures).

8. You would never see (deer), (baboons), or moose sniffing around the box.

9. Fine Greek (ladies) and (gentlemen) also knew to stay away.

10. In fact, all (people) of all social (classes) kept their distance when Agatha and Pantho arrived.

The missing parts of the chart have been filled in below.

Singular	Singular Possessive	Plural	Plural Possessive
berry	berry's	berries	berries'
cat	cat's	cats	cats'
desk	desk's	desks	desks'
dog	dog's	dogs	dogs'
family	family's	families	families'
glove	glove's	gloves	gloves'
house	house's	houses	houses'
Jones	Jones's	Joneses	Joneses'
peach	peach's	peaches	peaches'
thief	thief's	thieves	thieves'

The direct objects are circled and the indirect objects are underlined.

1. Zeus gave <u>Hera</u> her birthday *present*.

2. Hera thanked *him* over and over.

3. The special mirror gave <u>her</u> a real *thrill*.

4. She also showed her personal <u>attendant</u> this handmade *looking glass*.

5. Her servant admired *it* greatly.

The predicate nouns are underlined.

1. Cupid was the <u>god</u> of love.

2. Hercules was the strongest <u>resident</u> of Olympus.

3. The goddess of the hearth was <u>Hestia</u>.

4. She appears as the <u>subject</u> of very few stories.

5. The hearth was the <u>spot</u> where she remained.

The correct pronouns are underlined.

One day, when the sixth grade class was studying mythology, the students looked up at their teacher, Mr. Epstein. (<u>They</u>, Them) wanted to know what (<u>he</u>, him) thought of the Greek gods.

Jeff said, "Mr. Epstein, believe (I, <u>me</u>), we're not trying to get out of writing our in-class report. But please tell (we, <u>us</u>) which god is your favorite."

"Well, Jeff," replied Mr. Epstein, "let (I, <u>me</u>) think a minute. I don't like war, so I won't pick Ares or anyone like (he, <u>him</u>). Since my hobby is scuba diving, (<u>I</u>, me) am going to go with Poseidon, god of the sea."

"And your favorite goddess?" asked Stephanie. "(<u>We</u>, Us) kids are thinking you'll pick Athena because (<u>she</u>, her) is wise like you."

"Just between you and (I, _me_)," laughed Mr. Epstein, "I think men and women who handle love well are the wisest of all. Let (I, _me_) vote for Aphrodite."

"Terrific," said Stephanie. "I'll make a poster with drawings of both of (they, _them_) on it! Where are my Magic Markers?"

The correct relative pronouns are underlined.

1. Athens, (_which_, that) is the main city in Greece, is named for Athena.

2. Athena, (_who_, whom) was the goddess of wisdom, often had an owl with her.

3. Owls (which, _that_) lived in the Temple of Athena were very fortunate.

4. Athena was the goddess for (who, _whom_) a large statue was made.

5. (_Who_, Whom) has seen a picture of the building called the Parthenon?

The incorrect pronouns have been replaced.

1. Either Mackenzie or Lana was sure to have brought <u>her</u> new bathing suit.

2. <u>Those</u> who have read The Diary of Anne Frank know that they have read a classic.

3. "If <u>you</u> find a way out of the maze, would <u>you</u> please let us know?" cried the court jester.

4. "Oh, Brad," called Ms. Gioia, "neither Gaston nor you are able to figure out what <u>he</u> really <u>wants</u>."

5. "All of <u>us</u> are happy as clams at high tide to be here. We want to stay at this camp forever," cried Jenna.

The correct verbs are underlined.

1. Haley (cook, <u>cooks</u>) for the kids every night.

2. Every night, she (make, <u>makes</u>) their favorite meal: meatloaf.

3. "(Wasn't, <u>Weren't</u>) we going to have something different tonight, Haley?" (ask, <u>asks</u>) Sherman.

4. "Yikes! Meatloaf again!" (cries, <u>cry</u>) Catherine and Emily. "What about us vegetarians?"

5. "(Doesn't, <u>Don't</u>) you people have anything better to do than worry about dinner?" (wonder, <u>wonders</u>) Haley.

6. "Oh, I (<u>am</u>, is) sick of trying to please all of you whiners!" Haley says, as she (pull, <u>pulls</u>) her cookbook out of the drawer once again.

The verbs you should have changed to past tense are shown in italics. Make your own defense of the version you prefer.

One day in an ancient land, a sculptor named Pygmalion *decided* to create a statue of a beautiful woman. He *bought* a large block of the finest Parian marble and brought it to his workshop. Using all his skill, he *began* to shape it from an oblong block into the form of a human. Day and night he *worked*, and slowly the cold marble took on the shape of a woman. Pygmalion *could* hardly believe his skill *had* been able to bring forth such beauty.

Strangely enough, he *began* to fall in love with the statue. He *brought* gifts—a nosegay of violets, an amber necklace, a broken shell of a robin's egg—and *offered* them to it (or "her," as he was beginning to think of the statue).

"Dear goddess of love," he *prayed* one night, "please grant me this one favor. Could you give life to my creation?"

And as he *watched* in amazement, the pale white cheeks of the marble image *turned* pink with life, and the rigid statue *started* to bend toward him with a kiss!

(Almost two thousand years later, a British playwright named George Bernard Shaw *gave* the name *Pygmalion* to his play about a professor of linguistics who *transformed* a nearly illiterate young woman, Eliza Doolittle, into someone who *could* be mistaken for a princess. Perhaps you know some songs from the musical version called *My Fair Lady*?)

QUIZ #26: TENSES

The correct verb tense has been filled in each blank.

1. Yesterday, Aloyisius <u>ate</u> twenty-seven chocolate chip cookies. (to eat)

2. Before he ate the cookies, he <u>baked</u> four dozen. (to bake)

3. Right now, Spearminta <u>is chewing</u> her favorite chewing gum. (to chew)

4. Tomorrow, Phileas and Passepartout <u>will go</u> to Tasmania. (to go)

5. By next Wednesday, Jerome <u>will have read</u> a total of 10 books this summer. (to read)

6. Herman's collection of Popsicle sticks <u>won</u> second prize in the world competition. (to win)

7. Dave and Lisa's productivity <u>dropped</u> after they stopped dating. (to drop)

8. Johnny Johnson was sent to jail after he <u>threatened</u> to take over Jimmy's empire. (to threaten)

9. After he had wondered why everyone had giggled at him all day, Beth <u>told</u> Matthew that the class clown had taped the words "kick me" to the back of his sweater. (to tell)

10. Joe <u>builds</u> crazy gadgets out of duct tape and clay in his spare time.

The correct verb tenses are underlined.

1. Jake (<u>wept</u>, weeped) when he heard the bad news.

2. "My brother has (grew, <u>grown</u>)," he said.

3. "I have (laid, <u>lain</u>) on my bed too long!" she exclaimed.

4. "If I had (tore, <u>torn</u>) that piece of paper, no one would have found out."

5. "I (brang, <u>brought</u>) this on myself," thought Rosa.

6. Mr. Wysiwyg (<u>swore,</u> sworn) that his daughter Phoenicia would never marry an alligator wrestler.

7. Kurt Angle (hanged, <u>hung</u>) his Olympic gold medals on his bedroom wall.

8. Many competitors have (froze, <u>frozen</u>) in fear at the sight of Sackerson.

9. The match began when the timekeeper (<u>rang,</u> rung) the bell.

10. His confidence had been (<u>shaken,</u> shook) when the dodgeball referee ruled his lucky shorts too short.

Parentheses are around the participles.

1. When he discovered his (missing) barbecued ribs, Vince called for Linda.

2. Christian used the peaches (picked) from the tree to bake a pie.

3. Mr. Austin thought that Shane's answer was wrong because it included a (misspelled) word.

4. It is a great convenience to have (running) water.

5. There were so many (screaming) children in the movie.

The gerunds are underlined.

1. I always liked <u>playing</u> baseball.

2. We all enjoyed <u>running</u> out onto the field.

3.   <u>Batting</u> is the one thing I don't do well.

4.   <u>Fielding</u> is my area of expertise.

5.   <u>Winning</u> tournaments, however, is something everybody likes.

The infinitives are underlined.

1.   Michiko wanted <u>to see</u> the sights in Dallas.

2.   <u>To go</u> to the races was Nathan's favorite pastime.

3.   Mr. Settepane wanted <u>to dine</u> at his competitor's restaurant.

4.   Valerie hoped <u>to win</u> the track meet that week.

5.   Jerry always has <u>to run</u> from Tom after school.

6.   Ralph waits until the teacher is out of the room before he starts to eat his shoelaces.

7. "To work at the DMV is no picnic," Arlene said *to Max*. (Be sure you recognized that to Max is a prepositional phrase, not an infinitive.)

The correct adjective forms are underlined.

1. Of all the kids, Vernon was the (smarter, <u>smartest</u>).

2. Taylor was (<u>quieter</u>, quietest) than Jennifer.

3. Of the various popular snack foods, Harold likes pizza (better, <u>best</u>).

4. Nell and Cynthia are both odd, but Cynthia is the (<u>odder</u>, oddest).

5. Pierre is the (more, <u>most</u>) mysterious person I have ever met.

The correct modifiers are underlined.

1. Lucinda felt (<u>good</u>, well) on that (<u>beautiful</u>, beautifully) day.

2. Alex wanted (bad, <u>badly</u>) to call her and tell her how (<u>sad</u>, sadly) he felt.

3. Sydney told her sister that she dressed (good, <u>well</u>) for such a (<u>good</u>, well) day.

4. After coming to a (<u>sudden</u>, suddenly) stop, Lance's (<u>new</u>, newly) sports car screeched (loud, <u>loudly</u>).

5. Stomping (forceful, <u>forcefully</u>) out of the room, Leigh flipped her (<u>thick</u>, thickly) blonde hair out of her (<u>cool</u>, coolly) eyes.

The correct pronouns are underlined.

Hercules, the strong man of Mt. Olympus, was in a grumpy mood. (<u>He</u>, Him) couldn't decide what Zeus and the other gods thought of (he, <u>him</u>). So he decided to ask them. He believed Artemis, the goddess of hunting, admired both her brother Apollo and (he, <u>him</u>, himself). What, though, did Athena, the goddess of wisdom, think? He would check things out with both Artemis and (she, <u>her</u>).

"Hey, Artemis," he began, tossing his cloak of lion skin around his shoulders. "Give (I, <u>me</u>) a straight answer. What do you think of (I, <u>me</u>)?"

"People always ask (I, <u>me</u>) questions like this," she said, annoyed. "(<u>Who</u>, whom do they think they are?) But since it's you, Hercules, I'll answer. You're exactly the kind of guy I'd like to have go along on a hunt with my friends and (I, <u>me</u>, myself.) You're strong and capable. If I hurt (me, <u>myself</u>), I know you'd help. And (<u>who</u>, whom) has a cooler lion skin than you?"

"Thanks, Arty. Would Athena give you and (I, <u>me</u>) the same answer?"

"I'm not sure," said Artemis. "Why don't (<u>we</u>, us) curious Olympians go over to her place and ask (she, <u>her</u>, herself)?"

"Just between you and (I, <u>me</u>)," replied Hercules, "I'm a little scared of (she, <u>her</u>). Can you and (<u>I</u>, me) together be as intelligent as (<u>she</u>, her) is?"

"Everyone has different positive traits," Artemis replied. "Athena and (<u>I</u>, me) are different, but we get along.

Muster up your famous courage, and may no god bother you or (I, <u>me</u>) on the way there. To be certain, shall (<u>we</u>, us) just make (we, us, <u>ourselves</u>) invisible?"

The correct words are underlined.

"Good day, Athena," began Hercules. "I feel (<u>bad</u>, badly) to ask you this outright, but do you think I'm a cool guy?"

"Oh, Hercules, I'm the one who feels (<u>bad</u>, badly)," the goddess of wisdom wisely replied. "I've never seen you perform (bad, <u>badly</u>) at anything! I remember how you killed that fire-breathing bull, Cacus. I would have felt (<u>terrible</u>, terribly) if it had been the other way around. Did you bring Artemis with you to protect (you, <u>yourself</u>) from scary old (I, <u>me</u>)? Now that does make me feel (<u>bad</u>, badly)!"

The misplaced modifiers are underlined, and the rewritten sentences are below the original versions.

1. <u>Approaching his favorite television actor</u>, admiration was oozing out of Vincent.
   Approaching his favorite television actor, Vincent was oozing with admiration.

2. <u>Hearing the voice of her beloved</u>, a wave of excitement came over Lou.
   Hearing the voice of her beloved, Lou felt a wave of excitement.

3. <u>Riding in the back of the jeep</u>, the moon looked beautiful.
   Riding in the back of the jeep, the passengers thought the moon liked beautiful.
   or
   As they rode in the back of the jeep, the moon looked beautiful.

4. While kissing her, his wallet fell out of his back pocket.

While kissing her, he lost his wallet from his back pocket.

or

While he was kissing her, his wallet fell from his back pocket.

The corrected parallelisms are below.

1. Hercules was wearing a loincloth, a lion skin, and having goatskin sandals.
CORRECT: Hercules was wearing a loincloth, a lion skin, and goatskin sandals.

2. Athena tried to put him at ease in two ways: by complimenting him and she reminded him of how he defeated Cacus the bull.
CORRECT: Athena tried to put him at ease in two ways: by complimenting him and by reminding him of how he had defeated Cacus the bull.

3. After listening to the dialogue between Athena and Hercules, Artemis wondered whether to speak up and how she might begin.

   CORRECT: After listening to the dialogue between Athena and Hercules, Artemis wondered whether to speak up and how to begin.

4. Athena's robe pictured a scary image of the Gorgon Medusa, whose glance could turn a beast to stone or will threaten even a bold hero who stared at her too long.

   CORRECT: Athena's robe pictured a scary image of the Gorgon Medusa, whose glance could turn a beast to stone or threaten even a bold hero who stared at her too long.

5. Medusa's head was covered with clusters of serpents, both immature and adults.

   CORRECT: Medusa's head was covered with clusters of serpents, both immature and mature.

Corrections are in italics. Note: Some other corrections are possible. For example, you could say that John Steinbeck's list of prizes is a lot like *that of* (or *the list of*) William Faulkner.

John Steinbeck's list of prizes is a lot like William *Faulkner's*. They both won the Nobel Prize for Literature. By the way, did you like Steinbeck's *Of Mice and Men* more than any of *his other books*? Faulkner's style is not like *Steinbeck's*. It's *more* complicated and challenging to read.

QUIZ #38: SUBJECT-VERB AGREEMENT

Corrections are in italics.

The Parthenon, located on the high acropolis of Athens, is a very beautiful building. There *are* several features that make it so striking. Lining each side *are* several graceful columns. Inside the structure, framed by all those columns, *is* a large statue of Athena herself. Her reputation for wisdom and her skill in battle were behind her great popularity. The very word *Par-*

thenon, which comes from the classical Greek for "maiden," refers to the unmarried Athena.

The correct propositions are underlined.

1. The Greek hero Theseus went (<u>to</u>, by) the island of Crete to save people from a monster called the minotaur, who lived in the center of a maze.

2. The minotaur differed (<u>from</u>, with) many foes: He was half human, half bull.

3. Theseus was able to slay the minotaur and then find his way out of the maze with a thread he got (off of, <u>from</u>) Ariadne, the daughter of the king of Crete.

4. He must have been (<u>inside</u>, inside of) the maze for more than an hour.

5. (Beside, <u>Besides</u>) killing the minotaur, Theseus performed other valiant feats.

6. Shakespeare's use of Theseus as a character in his play A Midsummer Night's Dream was the result (<u>of</u>, from) centuries of retelling of stories about him.

The correct words are underlined.

1. Odysseus's trick on the Cyclops made that one-eyed giant so angry he was barely (intelligent, <u>intelligible</u>).

2. "(<u>Your</u>, You're) name is Noman?" said the Cyclops. "(Its, <u>It's</u>) the first time I've heard that name."

3. The Cyclops's brutal practice of eating men he disliked was more than (aggravating, <u>irritating</u>) to Odysseus.

4. The Greek hero remained in a (<u>stationary</u>, stationery) position in the Cyclops's cave to lessen the chances of being grabbed and consumed for dinner.

5. If Odysseus had lost (<u>fewer</u>, less) men to the Cyclops, he would have been happier.

6. "While I'd like to (<u>lie</u>, lay) down and nap," said Odysseus to himself, "I've got to think up a way to get out of this cave."

7. "Yes, (its, <u>it's</u>) true," said Odysseus later. "I (snuck, <u>sneaked</u>) out of the cave by holding on tightly to the fleece on the underbelly of a giant ram."

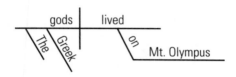

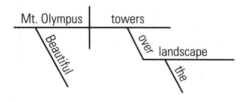

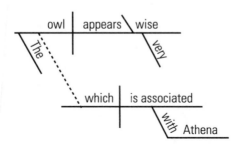

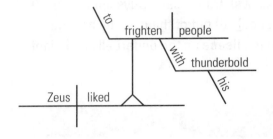

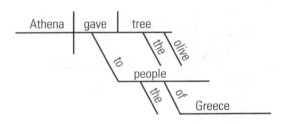

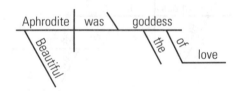

Added punctuation is in bold and underlined.

Our Greek wanderer Odysseus spent ten years fighting in Troy**,** and he also survived ten years of adventures trying to get back to Ithaca from Troy**,** which is in modern-day Turkey**.** The attempt to get home involved scary enemies such as these**:** jagged rocks**,** a whirlpool**,** a shipwreck**,** and beautiful mermaids who hoped to make him forget about home**.**

Finally**,** he arrives back in Ithaca**.** Hoping to check out things in the kingdom before he reveals his identity**,** he disguises himself as a poor man**,** a wanderer**.** Also**,** of course**,** he is 20 years older**.**

Do you think this disguise will work**?** It isn't perfect**,** as we'll see**.**

Amazingly enough—or not—Odysseus is first recognized by his dog**!** His master has been away for 20 years**,** but his special doggy talents allow him to see through the disguise**.** Homer makes the dog very real**,** giving him a name**,** Argus**,** and informing us that he suffers from fleas**.** Odysseus is filled with emotion at seeing Argus**,** but he must not reveal his feelings**.**

In a second emotional scene, Odysseus's old nurse recognizes him; she had tended him as a child. While offering him traditional hospitality, she recognizes a scar that he got as a boy. A fierce boar had gouged him with its tusks. The astonished nurse does not know whether to call him "dear child" or "my master."

"I beg you, dear nurse," he whispers to her, "do not tell the others who I am."

"Dear boy, I will keep your secret," she replies, but, like Argus, she is filled with emotion.

Some of the final scenes are violent, but the reader is most touched by Odysseus's reunion with Penelope. Although his wife has been faithful to him for his 20 years' absence, she is a match for her husband in courage and cunning. To get him to prove his identity, she tells a lie about the very special bed he, long ago, had built for the two of them. You must read Book 23 of *The Odyssey* to learn about this bed, her lie, and his response.

Ultimately, though, we may imagine Odysseus uttering the famous sentiment: "There's no place like home!"

ABOUT THE AUTHORS

Liz Buffa joined The Princeton Review in 1989. She has taught classes in SAT, LSAT, GMAT, and SAT-II special subject tests. She is a graduate of Wellesley College and lives in Locust Valley, New York, with her husband and two sons, David and Paul. This is her third book for The Princeton Review.

Jane Mallison has taught English to students in the seventh through twelfth grades for over a quarter of a century and describes herself as someone who loves to learn and loves to teach. She has a master's degree from Duke University and lives in Manhattan. She has also written a book about 120 "good reads" and has coauthored a vocabulary book.

NOTES

NOTES

NOTES

NOTES